• HALSGROVE DISCOVER SERIES ➤

UNUSUAL RAILWAY PUBS
REFRESHMENT ROOMS AND ALE TRAINS

BOB BARTON

W0010054

HALSGROVE

First published in Great Britain in 2013
Copyright © Bob Barton 2013

Title page photograph: *George V Refreshment Room, Horsted Keynes*

British Library Cataloguing-in-Publication Data
A CIP record for this title is available from the British Library

ISBN 978 0 85704 173 9

HALSGROVE
Halsgrove House,
Ryelands Business Park,
Bagley Road, Wellington, Somerset TA21 9PZ
Tel: 01823 653777   Fax: 01823 216796
email: sales@halsgrove.com

Part of the Halsgrove group of companies
Information on all Halsgrove titles is available at: www.halsgrove.com

Printed in China by Everbest Printing Co Ltd

Opposite: *Dingwall, north of Inverness, has both a traditional tea-room, seen at the far end of the station building of 1886, and a spacious on-platform pub, the Mallard. A Class 158 diesel unit for Kyle of Lochalsh enters on 1 June, 2012 (see page 142).*

CONTENTS

Stanier 8F No.8624 storms over the Caldon Canal and past the Black Lion on the delightful Churnet Valley Railway on 21 July, 2010. (see page 72).

ACKNOWLEDGEMENTS

I OWE A HUGE DEBT of gratitude to several people. Neil Wooler, former Public Affairs Manager for Travellers Fare, the catering arm of British Rail, allowed me unbridled access to his archive and read through the historical chapters. Our extended lunch meetings in railway pubs were particularly enjoyable. The patient reading of gazetteer entries by David A. Lawrence, MBE, former Property Director, British Rail Property Board, with his encyclopaedic knowledge of stations, has been invaluable. Michael Slaughter has suggested entries and contributed some excellent photographs. My family has put up with my long hours at the computer and casting of books and papers all over the house; Caroline and Joanna still seem to like their dad despite being taken to numerous stations and pubs on the pretext of a 'fun day out'!

Six years spent visiting locations and events has been at its most pleasant when in the company of friends, of which I only have space to mention James Young, Richard Tippett, Andrew Daines and Jeremy Brinkworth. Among those who also suggested pub entries were John Reeves, Nick Catford, Roy Lambeth and many readers of *Beer* magazine (Winter 2009 edition). John Owen, archivist at Shepherd Neame, has assisted on the subject of brewery transport. The patience of archivists including Elaine Arthurs of 'Steam' Museum, Swindon; those at the National Railway Museum, York and in local studies sections of numerous public libraries, was invaluable. Last but not least I pay tribute to the staff, managers and owners of the establishments featured herein, who work long, anti-social hours providing bonhomie and hospitality to complete strangers such as myself, and do their bit to maintain Britain's unique railway and pub heritage. *Bob Barton*

PHOTOGRAPHIC CREDITS

All photographs are by the author, or from his collection, except the following, courtesy of:

Nigel Shaw: 4.
Neil Wooler collection/Travellers Fare: 14, 17, 18 (top and middle), 20, 21, 22, 23 (top and middle), 24, 47 (lower), 94 (lower).
STEAM, Museum of the GWR, Swindon: 12.
National Railway Museum/NMSI: 16, 18 (bottom).
The Magic Attic, Swadlincote: 28.
Shepherd Neame Ltd. Archive: 31.
TfL, London Transport Museum collection: 41 (left).

Camden Local Studies and Archives: 44.
Matt Allen: 51.
Colour-Rail: 54 (upper), 55 (lower), 65 (upper).
Michael Slaughter LRPS: 60 (upper), 86 (upper), 92 (lower), 96 (upper), 111 (upper).
North Staffordshire Railway Co. (1978) Ltd: 72 (top).
M&GN Trust, M&GN Circle Photo Archive: 75 (main).
Cumbrian Railways Association collection: 80.
George William Robin: 92 (upper).

Pump clips and bottle label illustrations are courtesy of the breweries with further thanks to John Austin FGRA and the Kent & East Sussex Railway. Every effort has been made to contact copyright holders and we apologise for any unintentional omissions which will be rectified in future editions.

INTRODUCTION

'IF THOSE SANDWICHES were made this morning, then you're Shirley Temple!' So joke two young servicemen to the refreshment room manageress in the 1945 film *Brief Encounter.* It sums up the public attitude to the standard of catering in station refreshment rooms which persisted for decades, until comparatively recently.

How times have changed – if you know where to look. It is ironic that the re-created Brief Encounter buffet at Carnforth, Lancashire, a key location of the film, far from being an object of ridicule serving curling ham sandwiches or a warm pint of mild, is now a destination of choice. Romanticized through the rose-tinted optics of nostalgia, Carnforth's recreated buffet attracts hundreds of visitors. They come to enjoy lunch or afternoon tea, yards from the clock where the film's couple, played by Celia Johnson and Trevor Howard, parted after their trysts.

Other station refreshment rooms and pubs, once dreary and run-down, have now been restored to their Victorian or Edwardian splendour and serve imaginative selections of micro-brewery ale, British and foreign craft beers, good wine and filter coffee. Yet another type of hostelry featured in these pages I call the 'phoenix arisen'. These are historic buildings whose railway use finished decades ago as the network was being pruned. Far-sighted business people have adapted them to serve as a bar or tea-shop, giving new life to the structures and enjoyment to the public.

People's affection for railways is palpable and far-reaching. Though often based on nostalgia, it embraces all generations. Walking or cycling former lines is popular; so is riding steam and vintage diesel trains on main-line excursions and the increasing variety of heritage railways. The national network, though standardized, rationalized and reduced in size, still has much of interest including impressive bridges and viaducts, traditionally worked signal boxes and semaphore signalling, and a stunning array of architecture. Passengers are increasing: in 2011 it was announced by the train operators' association that the number travelling was the highest since 1923 – the year of the grouping into the 'Big Four', the GWR, LMS, LNER and SR.

The Number One, Cleethorpes, sported this attractive inn sign in 2006.

Some of the best places in which to soak up railway atmosphere are pubs and refreshment rooms. What could be better than sitting with a pint of ale, glass of wine or cup of fresh coffee in a place brimming with the essence and nostalgia of the iron road? It could be an ornate 'palace', once used by first class passengers awaiting famous named expresses, or the refreshment room on a provincial station where tank engines once simmered with workaday push-pull services. When I tried to obtain a guide to these places, I found none. So I decided to write one and this is it!

I had tremendous fun visiting and travelling to the establishments featured – mostly by train but also by bicycle, bus, on foot and, occasionally, by car. I sincerely hope you will too. Wherever appropriate I have also ridden heritage railways; and, quite by accident, a so-called 'ghost train' (Stockport to Stalybridge) and used a 'ghost station' (Gainsborough Central) on the national network, where normal daily services have been discontinued.

This book is divided into two main parts. Before visiting these places of hospitality, I explore the history of the subject. Today's pubs have evolved as they have partly thanks to the railways. In the early days of travel, trains didn't carry refreshments on board so a way had to be found to efficiently slake passengers' hunger and thirst *en route* to their destinations.

The railways took the concept of a place of refreshment for travellers and moulded it into something more in tune with the age and, sometimes, more decorative too – especially for those lucky enough to travel first class – with ornate woodwork and ceilings, mirrors and shelves well stocked with spirits. Nothing could compete with the best of these decoratively, other than the extravagant 'palace' pubs found in London and other major cities. This genre was later taken to a more decadent level by the 'gin palaces' in many cities. In smaller places the railway pub or refreshment room was much more basic – Spartan even – but what it lacked in ostentation it made up for as a hub of the community it served.

Railways are all about journeys and this book first takes you to Britain's past places of refreshment, before inspiring you

A traditional inn sign above the station platform is just one of this pub's unusual features. Railwayman's Arms, Bridgnorth Station, Shropshire.

(hopefully) to make your own trips to remarkable hostelries that serve today's traveller. Places where you can *celebrate* railways with a favourite drink, accompanied by generous portions of atmosphere and lashings of nostalgia.

1. ORGANIZED CHAOS

Refreshment stops on the early railways

THE PROLIFIC PEN of Charles Dickens was responsible for many memorable characters. They include Oliver Twist who nervously 'asked for more'; the cold-hearted Estella from *Great Expectations* and the affected humbleness of Uriah Heep in *David Copperfield*. To that merry band one should add a certain female: Our Missis, a formidable matron in charge of the Refreshment Room in *Mugby Junction,* a series of short stories published in 1866. Dickens – a determined rail traveller who was reputedly once treated in an off-hand way at Rugby – includes a thinly-disguised satire of that station's facilities in *The Boy at Mugby*. Using a young employee as his mouthpiece, he sums up the sad state of railway station catering. The proudest boast of the refreshment room is that it 'has never yet refreshed a mortal being' and the traveller will inevitably have his request for a drink met by an assistant who will 'appear in an absent manner to survey the line through a transparent medium composed of your head and body'.

Our Missis trains her staff to be as unhelpful and slothful as possible – to the extent that 'Other Refreshment Rooms send their imperfect young ladies up to be finished off' by her. Impatient, thirsty travellers are there to be ignored and tormented in equal measure. The fare is stale pastry and sawdust sandwiches, washed down with a liquid supposed to be either tea or soup 'according to the last twang imparted to the contents' of the tea-urn that doubles as a soup-tureen. The author's irony extends to his description of a 'sawdust department' where sandwiches are prepared. Dickens does not comment on the quality of the beer. Presumably, as it is bottled, it is deemed acceptable. The sherry however, then a more popular drink than it is today, can hardly be mentioned without a giggle.

By the time *Mugby Junction* was written, the railway network was already well established. The Liverpool & Manchester, the world's first timetabled passenger line, had opened more than 30 years previously, in 1830. We have to go further back to see how inns were more than just places of refreshment but fundamental to the development of railways.

Before lines could be built, crucial meetings were held between businessmen and other local worthies, to hammer out proposals and routes, agree funding and apply for parliamentary approval. Where better to bring local parties together than in the convivial setting of the local inn? After two attempts to promote a railway from the South Durham coalfields were defeated in parliament, a meeting in the George & Dragon public house in Yarm in February 1820, chaired by the charismatic Thomas Meynell, Squire of Yarm, agreed to press for a third bill. It was to prove third time lucky and led to the building of the world's first public railway, the Stockton & Darlington. A plaque outside commemorates the event and is tactile proof that one of the most important meetings in the history of railways happened in a pub.

There are many other examples of debates about proposed railways taking place in inns. Fans of the Midland Railway pay homage to one in Nottinghamshire that still functions as a busy hotel and hostelry. Meetings at the Sun Inn in Eastwood led to the foundation of the Midland Counties Railway, one of the three companies that were to form the mighty Midland. Author D.H. Lawrence, who grew up locally and was an inveterate rail traveller, mentions the establishment in his autobiographical *Sons and Lovers*. At another literary centre, Haworth in West Yorkshire, once home to the Brontë sisters, their brother

Branwell spent many hours carousing in the Black Bull Inn. Less well known is that formal gatherings here led to the building of a line justly popular with steam enthusiasts today: the Keighley & Worth Valley.

Before the railways, the fastest form of public transport was the stage-coach. The tradition of staging inns developed – many of them built specially for the purpose – to serve as 'pit-stops' for both passengers and horses. Both required feeding and watering, while passengers on longer routes needed overnight accommodation, and horses had to be changed at frequent intervals. The catering requirements for a stage-coach and its mere dozen or so passengers and those of a train, often with several hundred on board, were vastly different. But the railway planners had no other infrastructure on which to base their customer facilities.

So, as the first public railways opened, it seemed only natural that they should follow the traditions of the stage-coach. For years, the trains of the Liverpool & Manchester line were despatched 'by a lively tune performed by a trumpeter at the end of the platform,' just as a bugle-call announced arrival and departure of the coach-and-four. Inns were often used as both waiting rooms and ticket offices on the early lines, so the

Plaque marking the site of the Royal Hotel, an early booking office for the Liverpool & Manchester Railway, in Market Street, Manchester.

concept of having a pint while awaiting your train is as old as the railways themselves. The L&M's first booking office, and place where passengers boarded coaches to the railhead, was the Royal Hotel in central Manchester. Though this hostelry and Royal Mail staging post no longer stands, there is a plaque on the site, 124-130 Market Street. On the Stockton & Darlington, opened five years earlier and where the trains were often horse-drawn, coaching inns were not only ticket agents but provided many facilities later found at stations.

When companies started building stations at intermediate calling points, the provision of refreshments was not a priority. There is some debate as to which was the first inn built for, and owned by, a railway company. The Gartsherrie Inn, opened in 1832 at the country end of the little-known Garnkirk & Glasgow Railway is a contender. This far-sighted company realised that sightseers, using the coal-carrying line for a day out from Glasgow, had to await a return train with nothing but coal-tips to admire, so they commissioned the 'commodious inn [where] every convenience is afforded'. These 'conveniences' only survived until 1843, when the inn closed and the building was demolished in the 1960s.

Earlier, at least one horse-drawn tramway also built a hostelry. This was the Tram Inn of 1829 near Didley, Herefordshire, between Pontrilas and Hereford. It was constructed for and owned by the Hereford Railway Company, being a combined station and inn until 1855 when a purpose-built station opened on what was to become the Newport, Abergavenny & Hereford Railway.

The dearth of refreshments on the first railways was filled, as it was for the stage-coaches before, by local entrepreneurs. On the route of the former Liverpool & Manchester is a hostelry claimed to be the world's first pub built for trade from a railway. Originally the Patricroft Tavern, later the Queen's Arms, it stands beside the tracks by Patricroft Station, near Eccles, and was built in 1828. Such was the confidence of its sponsor that it not only opened two years before the railway it was intended to serve but is sited away from the village centre, on a dead-end driveway above the main road (and is still known locally as the

The Queen's Arms, originally the Patricroft Tavern, beside Patricroft Station, dates from 1828 and was the first pub built for trade from railway passengers.

'Top House'). Its place in history was assured, and its name changed, following a train-borne visit by Queen Victoria and Prince Albert in 1857. The royal couple disembarked here to continue their journey by canal barge, sailing to Worsley Hall, where they were entertained by the Duke of Bridgewater. Awarded Grade II listing after representations by the Campaign for Real Ale (CAMRA), the simple, slate-roofed pub retains its original four-roomed layout, complete with snug, real fires and etched glass: an atmospheric survivor.

The L&M was surprised by the popularity of its first trains among a public eager to experience the novelty of 'high-speed'

travel. The regular movement of goods was postponed for months in order to satisfy the demands of passengers wanting to journey between the two cities in a fraction of the four-and-a-half hours taken by coaches. Local businessmen near the termini had a field-day, with rail travellers soon being enticed by advertisements for 'home-brewed ale', 'old wines' and 'well-aired beds'. Local taverns en route sent their staff out to meet trains, hawking liquor, ale, cigars and snacks, such as the local delicacy Eccles cakes, along the carriages. (Something that can still be experienced on train journeys in some developing countries, except for the Eccles cakes.) Delays soon occurred, so the company forbade the practice. The ruling was promptly ignored as, shortly after, a passenger reported encountering 'a local serving wench' walking beside the train at Patricroft with a large tray stocked with drinks, glasses and cigars, selling surreptitiously to first class passengers!

Binge drinking is not a modern phenomenon, and a problem for the early railways was that of passengers and others who had over-indulged in alcohol. On the L&M there are reports of an inebriated man being hit by a train after walking along the top of a rail, tight-rope fashion, in Liverpool's Olive Mount cutting. Another fell to his death from a second-class carriage near Bury Lane. Railway staff too, including enginemen, were often discovered drunk on duty.

COMPULSORY REFRESHMENT STOPS

As the network grew and the main lines were pieced together, it was necessary for the companies to introduce some order to the refreshment business. On-board catering had yet to develop, so the answer for longer journeys was a compulsory refreshment stop every 50 miles or so, at a station where suitable facilities could be provided. Trainloads of hungry and thirsty individuals then had ten minutes or so to grab the Victorian equivalent of a panini and a pint. Places like Carlisle, Swindon, Wolverton, Preston, York and (superior, by all accounts) Normanton near Leeds, where the Midland Railway's Scottish expresses paused to enable a *six course meal* to be served and eaten in 20 minutes, became the motorway service stations of their day. Imagine the chaos as hundreds of passengers made a mad dash for the bar to quickly buy and consume whatever they could. Before the whistle blew there was a mad dash in reverse and they were off again in a cloud of steam and smoke. Queen Victoria was not exempt, being forced to endure a stop in un-regal Wolverton during her first trip on the London and Birmingham Railway in 1843.

The scenes of chaos that ensued at these places engendered them with dreadful reputations that became bread-and-butter material for a generation of cartoonists and music-hall comedians. The incentive for food to be edible or staff to be courteous was probably non-existent, especially as they knew their customers would shortly vanish down the track. The invention of fast food restaurants, microwave ovens or cellophane, to keep food fresh, was still decades away. Catering on board trains was also some way off, the absence of carriages with connecting corridors being one of the hurdles to be overcome.

As early as 1862 *The Railway Traveller's Handybook* – a sort of early *Rough Guide* – was advising passengers to avoid 'overcrowded refreshment halts'. Dickens returned to his dislike of these establishments in *The Uncommercial Traveller*, where he speaks of a 'depressing banquet on the table' and being offered 'brown hot water stiffened with flour', 'and glutinous lumps of gristle and grease called pork pie.' He wasn't the only author who scorned railway fare – in 1868 Anthony Trollope, in *He Knew He Was Right*, announced that the railway sandwich was 'the real disgrace of England.'

The London & Birmingham Railway (later the London & North Western) can boast the earliest station refreshment rooms, around the time of the line's opening in 1838. These were at Rugby (where passengers for a time changed to a road coach) and, more grandly, as part of a licensed hotel set up at its Birmingham Curzon Street terminus. This was indeed posh, boasting a panelled ceiling and two rows of Corinthian columns. In September 1838 *The Times* reported that 'the station house has recently been licensed as a hotel...passengers, if they think proper, may be accommodated with every good thing without leaving the company's premises.' In fact every convenience was thought of, quite literally, in the early days of railways: it was stations that provided the first public toilets, and the phrase to 'spend a penny' was coined. Part of Curzon Street survives and is Grade I listed, though sadly not the hotel, nor train-shed, but is visible from trains approaching New Street Station from the south. It may one day be used again, for the proposed High Speed Two (HS2) line. Local innkeepers were most put out, complaining that the new hostelry held a monopoly over rail travellers.

It was the refreshment rooms at the halfway point of

Wolverton, opened the same year – where passengers had a few minutes' to join a scrum in order gain sustenance – that got most attention. Wolverton, in rural Buckinghamshire, was a new town created by the railway. A description written in 1849 by diplomat turned essayist Francis Bond Head, titled *Stokers and Pokers,* describes the rooms as being run by a group which included '...a matron or *generalissimo* in charge of seven very young waitresses, a man-cook, kitchen-maid, two scullery maids, two laundry-maids, a baker, and an "odd-man".' There was also livestock in the form of 85 pigs and 'piglings'. These, he was at pains to observe '... are most kindly treated and luxuriously fed, are impartially promoted, by seniority, one after another into an infinite number of pork pies.'

It goes on to explain how 'youthful handmaidens standing in a row behind bright silver urns' manage to serve, quickly and with minimal exchange of words, an endless combination of tea, coffee, soup, cakes, buns and 'lady's fingers', while other staff are:

'Rapidly uncorking, and then emptying into large tumblers, innumerable black bottles of what is not inappropriately called Stout... in fact they are *very* stout. But the bell is violently calling the passengers to Come! Come away! ...as the engine is loudly hissing... they soon like the swallows of summer, congregate together and fly away.'

On the Great Western, Isambard Kingdom Brunel's refreshment rooms at Swindon were opened in July 1842 and consisted of two large, three-storey stone buildings, one either side of the main line. The southern block was demolished in 1972 but the northern one remains, its interior completely changed. The basement of each contained kitchens, offices and attendants' rooms, while the ground floor was taken over by a large, lavishly decorated refreshment room divided into first and second class sections with an oval 'island' bar counter of marble in the middle. Third class passengers and working men were relegated to a separate building across the courtyard which survives as a pub, now the Queens Tap. Though the interior is totally altered and its outbuildings (which included stables)

At Swindon, the GWR opened some of the first railway refreshment rooms in 1842. This is a 1890s view of one of the first class rooms.

The Queen's Tap, built 1842-3 and still in business opposite Swindon Station, was where third class passengers were relegated, the railway equivalent of a coaching inn.

demolished, this too was part of the GWR's original Swindon refreshment set-up. The oldest pub in New Swindon with a full licence and Grade II listed, it is a rare survivor; the railway's equivalent of a coaching inn.

The GWR's directors probably thought they were clever when, in 1841, they signed a 99 year lease for the building of refreshment rooms at Swindon in exchange for an agreement to stop trains there for ten minutes and not build competing establishments along the line. It got the facility for nothing but it soon became a mill-stone. For the builders, Joseph and Charles Rigby, it was a gold-mine. For decades, passengers were held captive to some badly run catering facilities and, later, GWR expresses were slowed when other railway companies, who had also done catering deals but without such cast-iron agreements, were able to speed theirs up. After failing in legal attempts to wriggle out of the deal, the GWR finally bought out the lease in 1895 for an extortionate £100,000.

The reputation of the establishment was such that even Brunel, the railway's engineer, was forced to write in 1842 to the caterer regarding the coffee (the son of a Frenchman he was probably more irritated than most on this subject):

'Dear Sir, I assure you Mr Player was wrong in supposing that I thought you purchased inferior coffee. I thought I said to him that I was surprised you should buy such bad roasted corn. I did not believe you had such a thing as coffee in the place; I am certain that I never tasted any. I have long ceased to make complaints at Swindon. I avoid taking anything there when I can help it.'

The growing legions of railwaymen needed refreshment, too. So-called 'railway villages' were built by the big companies to house them at important route centres, such as Swindon and Derby. Licensed premises for their off-duty relaxation soon followed. The 'world's first purpose-built railwayman's inn', built in 1842, survives at Derby, while there are three pubs still at the heart of Swindon's village.

As railway companies developed ways of catering for large numbers of patrons they gave something to the catering industry that we take for granted today: the long bar counter.

Few pubs and inns in those days had such a thing as a counter. Instead, customers were served their jugs of ale by maids or pot boys – or even by the brewer him or herself – who fetched beer straight from the barrel, and served it at the table (an arrangement used today at two places featured in the Gazetteer which starts on page 39).

The counter was in use in gin shops by the early nineteenth century; pubs picked up on the idea but the railways perfected it. The long – sometimes straight, sometimes oval – counter where customers could order their drinks and food was established on stations in the 1840s as a way of speeding up customer service. This was seen first at Wolverton, where young waitresses lined up in a row behind an extended bar, attending to the advancing hordes with formalities reduced to a minimum. Swindon's refreshment rooms included their efficient oval bar counters; by 1879, Preston on the LNWR had a double-sided, or horseshoe shaped one. Aside from being rather elegant, this too allowed staff to serve the greatest number of people with the least amount of effort.

Towards the end of the century, many railway companies seemed to have got their act together. On the Highland Railway, where journeys from Perth to Inverness took in excess of five hours and those from Inverness to Wick at least seven (in carriages without corridors or toilets) refreshment rooms were built at Kingussie and Bonar Bridge respectively. Trains stopped for ten minutes, allowing passengers to collect their hot or cold food basket, complete with a small bottle of claret (passengers were allowed to send a free telegram to Kingussie reserving them) while Bonar Bridge was known for its bowls of steaming soup, all neatly laid out to meet train arrivals. Advancing passengers called out 'a sixpenny spoon, miss' paying their sixpences to obtain a spoon with which to consume the beverage displayed so enticingly.

Though compulsory refreshment stops died out in tandem with the increasing speed of crack expresses and the introduction of dining cars, the station refreshment room and its cousin, the station hotel or pub, entered a golden age of architectural magnificence. Polished mahogany woodwork and

This refreshment room at Colchester (down side) resembled scores of others on provincial stations, but it was considered distinctive enough to be shown on a sepia postcard sent in 1904. Note the Great Eastern Railway timetables displayed inside.

ornate ceramic tiles were used to create a palatial look, even if the food quality was still frequently the source of complaint.

Victorian and Edwardian society was class obsessed and, up until the 1920s, many stations had three refreshment rooms. First class was often spacious and palatial, as can still be seen at The Centurion at Newcastle Central, while second class was smaller (even though it handled larger numbers and was often crowded as a result). Third class travellers were, if they were lucky, given the equivalent of a bare, spit-and-sawdust bar or, as at Swindon, cast out of the station altogether.

As we have seen, some early station refreshment rooms had a poor reputation but the far-sightedness of three men, one

American and two British-born entrepreneurs who earned their fortunes in Australia, changed things forever. The American was George Mortimer Pullman, whose Pullman Palace Car Company signed a 15-year agreement with the Midland Railway. This led to U.S. Pullman cars being 'kit-built' using American components delivered to Derby, and the first hot meal being cooked and served on board a British train. This was a charter from London (St Pancras) to Wick and the year was 1878. Together with the advent of corridor trains, it was a revolutionary step. Station-based drinking and dining, which once had a captive customer base, had competition at last.

The two British gentlemen were Felix Spiers and Christopher Pond and their company, Spiers & Pond, shook up the refreshment business both on and off trains. The couple met in Australia, where they made their money feeding gold miners at hotels and their own Café de Paris in Melbourne (in 1861 they also brought over the first All-England cricket team). In England they are best known for opening the Criterion Restaurant at London's Piccadilly Circus, but they also realised there was scope for feeding the multitudes using British stations. Their first contract was for the Metropolitan Railway's Farringdon Street refreshment room in 1863, soon joined by a deal to run all the outlets on the London, Chatham & Dover Railway. Their empire mushroomed until it included the London & South Western, South Eastern, Lancashire & Yorkshire and North British Railways and the Cheshire Lines Committee. In 1871 they introduced the railway refreshment hamper, a meal picked up at the station for eating on the train, served in a recyclable basket which was handed in at journey's end; an idea soon copied by other companies. By 1929 they were running the Metropolitan's Chiltern Court Restaurant at Baker Street. Though now a pub (see page 41), it is not difficult to picture it with freshly laundered tablecloths and with waitresses in starched white outfits serving afternoon tea.

2. ALE AND HEARTY
The development of station pubs and buffet cars

AS THE RAILWAYS spread to every corner of the country, so almost every station sprouted a licensed refreshment room or an adjacent pub – sometimes both. The Railway, Railway Arms, Tavern or Hotel; The Station and The Locomotive are found everywhere. Unusual names such as The Atmospheric Railway Inn (Starcross, Devon) or The Branksome Railway (Branksome, Dorset) are rarer but their function is the same. Even the Necropolis Railway, which carried the coffins of the deceased together with mourners from a special station near London's Waterloo to the sprawling cemetery of Brookwood in Surrey until the early 1940s, considered the importance of alcoholic refreshment. Along with chaplains' rooms, mourners' waiting rooms and toilets, each of its two stations on the short line in the cemetery grounds contained a licensed refreshment room. Reputedly, there were signs on the bars declaring 'spirits served here'.

We've grown accustomed to being able to buy a beer or other alcoholic drink at almost any time but of course that wasn't always the case. Licensing laws were fairly liberal during the early days of railways, with customers only being denied access to pubs for a few days a year, such as Good Friday, Christmas Day and during the hours of church services on Sundays. Even these minimal restrictions could be avoided if the establishment was open 'for the refreshment of travellers', so railway locations were able to serve almost continuously. The Beer Act of 1830 had liberated the hours during which drink could be served, even allowing householders, on obtaining a licence, to brew and sell their own ale to passers-by if they wished. At the same time there was a move to limit the sale of alcohol. Bradford saw England's first temperance society in

The Railway Tavern at Reedham, Norfolk, was once home to the Humpty Dumpty brewery (see page 131).

1830 and two years later seven men committed themselves to total abstinence at another society in Preston. It was here that a subsequent member, a stammerer, reputedly gave the phrase 'tee-total' (abstinence) to the English language. It is worth noting that the first railway excursion, run by a Mr Thomas Cook in 1841, was a temperance one, a diversion from the temptation of alcohol. By the end of the nineteenth century 'demon drink' was being targeted as the cause of all society's ills. Pubs became places that 'gentlemen' didn't venture into. Licensing began to be restricted and, on the outbreak of World War I, the 1914 Defence of the Realm Act led, among other measures, to a drastic reduction in pub opening hours.

The Art Nouveau North Eastern Railway tea-room at York, seen from the platform soon after its 1906 opening. In 2011 it became a place of refreshment again. (see page 125).

Railway refreshment rooms offered the ideal loophole for those wishing to circumvent the restrictions. On Sundays particularly, buying a drink could be a problem and one way to get around the law was to buy a return rail ticket of at least three miles, enabling you to drink alcohol at the departure station and, if you actually took the train, at the arrival one too!

An alternative to the boozy refreshment room – and particularly popular with ladies – was the tea-room, encouraged by many railway companies in key locations, reaching its zenith in Edwardian times. An assortment of delicate sandwiches and cakes, made on the premises, would be served with tea or coffee on china crockery. One of the finest surviving architectural examples can be seen on York Station. Designed in the Art Nouveau style by William Bell and built in 1906 of wood with bay windows set with coloured glass, the North Eastern Railway's Tea Room and Café (set back from the main up platform adjacent to the hotel) was, and still is, an eye-catching feature. *Railway Magazine* of December, 1908 describes it as '...charmingly decorated in a kind of Oriental style...[it] supplies true North Country teas at moderate rates.' After many years of being used

for other things, the Tea Room became a 'craft beer house' in 2011, offering travellers hospitality once again.

BIRTH OF THE BUFFET CAR

For those who preferred refreshment of an alcoholic nature, there were increasing on-train alternatives to the station pub. Restaurant cars had started in 1879, with the Great Northern's *Prince of Wales,* a converted Pullman sleeper carriage. In 1881 the LBSCR's 'Pullman Limited Express' served buffet-style refreshments in former Midland Railway cars. Travelling pub-type bars available to all the passengers on a train had to wait until the turn of the century however, with the Great Central's revolutionary innovation, its Buffet Car, introduced for its new main line into London Marylebone. With an elegant, curved bar of polished mahogany, pub-type prints on the walls, a decorative ceiling and even gas cooking equipment so the attendant could rustle-up hot snacks, they were years ahead of their time. Not altogether successful, though: passengers were used to at-seat service in proper dining cars, rather than having to go up to a counter, so the vehicles were converted into conventional restaurant cars in 1907-8. But the die had been cast and, in 1908, the 'Southern Belle' – forerunner of the iconic 'Brighton Belle' – featured a bar and lounge-style seating in its parlour car *Belgravia*. Two years later, the Metropolitan Railway began running two Pullman buffet cars complete with a wooden bar counter at one end, a small kitchen behind, and one-plus-one armchair seating in glass-partitioned saloons. It was akin to a gentleman's club on wheels and sipping a gin and tonic in comfort while travelling home from the City to leafy Metro-Land is a pleasure today's Underground commuters can only dream of! The ultimate in on-train imbibing arrived in the late twenties when the LNER used an Art Deco poster to advertise cocktails served on the prestigious 'Flying Scotsman' to Edinburgh. This must have attracted passengers as, in 1932, the company saw fit to adapt the train's hairdressing carriages (yes, really!) to include a fully fledged cocktail bar. This innovation was also added to the competing LMS 'Coronation Scot' on the West Coast main line. By 1933, when Gresley introduced buffet cars on his third-class Tourist Stock, designed to compete with the long distance bus and coach operators, the revolution was complete.

It was during this halcyon pre-war period that the first attempts were made to create on-train versions of the pub, complete with that important pub staple, cask ale. In the mid-thirties the 'Garden Cities' and 'Cambridge Buffet Expresses'

Passengers relax in style beside an Art Deco cocktail bar as they speed north on the 'Coronation Scot' from London Euston in 1937.

Left: Scalloped tables, wall decoration and table lamps add a touch of class to this rebuild of a 1938 Bognor buffet car, seen in 1967. The '4 Buf' units were originally decorated in pastel shades, with a royal blue Wilton carpet, while the exterior was in the Southern Railway's malachite green.

Below: In the words of the press release: '...the traditional style of an old English tavern.' Oliver Bulleid's unusual Tavern Cars were introduced on BR's Eastern and Southern Regions in 1949. Real ale was served, in glass jugs too, but they received a mixed welcome.

Bottom: Exterior of a Bulleid Tavern Car on the 'Atlantic Coast Express'. The bizarre pub styling included individual painted inn signs: this example was 'The Jolly Tar'.

between King's Cross and Cambridge gained a popular reputation among ale-swilling undergraduates and were a foretaste of the real ale trains now run on many heritage railways. The students who then, as now, didn't seem short of a bob or two for alcohol, dubbed them the 'beer trains'. The Southern Railway, with its shorter main-line runs, also experimented with buffet configurations, such as the Bognor buffet cars which had both a long bar counter and draught ale as well as bottled. The more liberal licensing laws applying to moving trains were an incentive and, in 1964, this liberalization was extended further when the Licensing Act permitted full exemption from licensing laws to railway vehicles, providing food was also served.

World War II, with its food shortages and rationing, saw the start of a steady decline in dining car services and patronage but the buffet car saw a corresponding rise in sales. In 1946-7 Oliver Bulleid designed his somewhat bizarre Tavern Cars for the Southern Railway and these opened for business under the new British Railways banner in 1949. Though the idea was well-intentioned, they were something of an abomination. Their exteriors – to be precise, *half* their exteriors – carried pretend brickwork, half-timbering and even a painted-on pub sign with names such as 'White Horse', 'Green Man' and, appropriately, 'Bull', but anyone who believed this looked like a pub would have had to be fairly intoxicated. Stepping inside, the fantasy continued with wood panelling, an 'oak-beamed' ceiling, lanterns with frosted glass and pew-type seating. On the plus side, the ale was served from the cask in proper glass jugs. The draught beer of choice – certainly on the Southern – was Ind Coope & Allsopp's Bitter but author Neil Wooler remembers the quantity of beer sold was measured using a home-made wooden dipstick and '...problems arose with the motion of the train – especially across all those junctions on Southern lines – which made for a very murky pint.'

Murky ale or not, a journey on board a train such as the 'Atlantic Coast Express' from London Waterloo to Cornwall with one of these carriages in the consist, would have been an experience to savour. On this service at least the vehicles were popular and reportedly enjoyed the best turnover of all railway catering vehicles of the time, but they did not find favour generally with travellers. This was partly because they only had narrow, frosted windows which were almost impossible to see out of. On the Eastern Region the Tavern Cars attracted the attention of the temperance lobby and Methodist Church who opposed rolling stock that not only looked like a pub but also had the temerity to serve alcohol without food. The subject was discussed in the House of Commons; letters of complaint penned to *The Times* and, in 1959, they were converted into standard BR Mark I buffet cars. But the railways realised that alcohol sales, particularly beer, was a profit-maker, while on-train food sales made a loss. Alcohol consumption without food would never be restricted, except on trains for football fans.

The carriage that evolved to serve the needs of a whole generation of travellers was the BR Mark I Restaurant Miniature Buffet (RMB), a large number of which were built from the late 1950s until 1962. In the space usually occupied by a few seats, the designers managed to fit a fully-stocked bar, a circulating space and shelves for passengers' drinks. Many

BR's Mark I Restaurant Miniature Buffet (RMB), is arguably the most successful post-war catering vehicle, with many still in use on heritage railways. This view of BR No.1869, built at Wolverton in 1961, on the Kent & East Sussex Railway in June 2010, demonstrates the efficient use of limited servery space for product storage and kitchen facilities, including a water boiler.

readers will recall journeys which included at least one visit to one of these busy buffets, standing in a queue watching the attendant juggle with cool drinks, sandwiches, hot pies and teas and coffees supplied from a propane gas-fired boiler, all in a miniscule space.

A pub-style carriage resurfaced in 1961 in the form of the much admired Griddle Car, which became a regular fixture on services such as those between Edinburgh and Inverness. Two curving banks of soft upholstered seats created a comfortable and informal environment, while drinks and snacks were served

Military uniforms are in evidence in this 1940 photograph showing the buffet bar at London St Pancras equipped with a temporary booking office. The official one was out of action after bomb damage.

from a bar supplied from a central kitchen. The latter included a propane gas 'griddle' hot plate where an Aberdeen Angus steaklet in a bread roll could be rustled up in two minutes for one-and-ninepence (less than ten pence), a tasty accompaniment to your beer or whisky.

The fortunes of station-based refreshment rooms and pubs were also mixed. Pre-war, while 1930s drinkers supped cocktails in style on board the 'Flying Scotsman' or 'Coronation Scot', travellers could indulge in ales and spirits, pastries, pies and coffee served on GWR crockery while perched on shiny stools at the Art Deco-style Quick Lunch and Snack Bar at London's Paddington terminus. The spirit of places like this, right down to similar crockery, has been re-kindled at Birmingham Moor Street (see page 57). With the outbreak of World War II, those days of elegance would disappear. Scores of establishments closed completely and those that remained were constantly crowded and short of supplies. The Blitz caused greater mayhem – a bomb fell through the roof of the dining room, thankfully empty at the time, at King's Cross – and a wartime photograph shows the buffet bar at London St. Pancras multi-tasking as a temporary ticket office.

Food rationing, which continued until the early 1950s, also contributed to a general downhill trend in the quality of station pubs. People deserted the railways in the post-war period, thanks to the rise of the motor-car and an expanding and improving road network. Many station refreshment rooms fell into decline through lack of patronage. Roadside inns, many of which had suffered when railways killed the stage-coach business, saw a resurgence from the growth of leisure motoring.

The 1945 David Lean film *Brief Encounter*, based on a Noel Coward play about a couple's romantic trysts, brought tears to the eyes of war-weary cinema goers. Much of it was set in a station refreshment room which epitomised the state of these places at the time. Plain, drab and often run along quasi-military lines by formidable females, they were not places in which to linger.

DECLINE, THEN A RAIL AND ALE REVIVAL

Increasing line closures in the 1950s and sixties, epitomized by the Beeching cuts of the latter decade, and the British Rail 'modernization' period which followed into the seventies, did no favours to the quality of station drinking and dining. Architectural features on and around stations were seen as old-fashioned and expensive to maintain and promptly boarded-up, disguised or demolished. The curling BR sandwich and rock-hard pork pie became a national joke.

That said, many station pubs managed to create a pleasant ambience, were held in high regard by their customers, and much loved like many other 'locals'. Even at remote junction stations, like the lonely outpost of Barmouth Junction (now Morfa Mawddach) on the west coast of Wales, the refreshment room, on the island platform, doubled as the local pub. Station

An immaculate Crewe refreshment room, on platforms 3/4, about 1952 shows an establishment whose plentiful stock includes casks of Ind Coope & Allsopp ale and a window-mounted 'drinks indicator' showing Younger's, Arctic and Tolly ales and 'by golly it does you good' Mackeson's stout for sale.

This elegant Tudor-style refreshment room, part of Sir William Tite's Carlisle Citadel Station, seen in 1953, served its last customer long ago (though the buffet on platforms 2/3 is still in business). A fireplace inscription in Latin translates as 'I will make you always remember this place'.

staff and locals alike would down their drinks as they joined in some hearty choral singing: the melodic sounds of this impromptu male-voice choir drifting across an otherwise silent estuary. Railway authors David St John Thomas and Patrick Whitehouse recall another golden memory of the station in *The Great Days of the Country Railway:*

'It was not uncommon to see the driver descend from his Dean 0-6-0 or Cambrian goods...walk up and down the train for prying eyes and nip into the rooms for a pint of ale. He was soon joined by the guard (discipline required the fireman to remain on the footplate) along

with one or two passengers. After voices had been suitably lubricated, a good sing-song competed with the engine's safety valve, the driver assuring passengers that it would not leave without him.'

A similar tale would have been repeated on a hundred different branch lines up and down the land in the days of steam. Thomas and Whitehouse again:

'...At almost every junction and town of importance, there was the welcoming, always warm refreshment room. Never did orangeade quench the thirst so thoroughly as that on the station on the marshes at

Most station refreshment rooms are subject to regular makeovers. These three images show how changing fashions have been reflected in the exterior of the concourse bar at Glasgow Queen Street. The first two were taken before and after a 1949 rebuilding, while the third is the current incarnation, as Bonapartes, taken in 2011. Today's interior décor reflects the city's Art Nouveau heritage. Customers are now encouraged to sit 'outside', under the graceful train shed roof, watching trains being prepared for Edinburgh and West Highland line departures.

Dovey Junction or, a decade earlier (when they first came off the ration) biscuits hit the spot so satisfactorily as during an early morning change at Bodmin Road' (now Bodmin Parkway).

The so-called Beeching axe – the cuts in the railway network following Dr Richard Beeching's (then Chairman of British Railways) 1963 report *The Reshaping of British Railways* – hastened refreshment room closures. Between 1954 and 1966 a hundred disappeared, including establishments on lonely junctions which ceased to be so (Barmouth Junction was one); old fashioned dining rooms on quite large stations and friendly buffets in rural outposts. At the same time, many an adjacent Railway Arms and Station Tavern lost its *raison d'etre* and found itself marooned, all-but-forgotten in an empty approach road beside derelict, weed-filled platforms.

The 1973 oil crisis brought an end to large-scale rail closures and in the same year British Rail Catering gave itself the new, trendy name Travellers-Fare, a moniker selected by customers from a marketing consultant's list of suggestions. It promptly gained a five million pound grant from BR for a huge renovation programme which would have mixed blessings for its patrons.

Makeovers were nothing new, of course and Travellers-Fare went gung-ho with melamine finishes and large plastic lampshades in poster-paint colours. This echoed an earlier 'brave new look' which British Transport Catering Services had promoted in a booklet *The Hungry Traveller* in 1953. This explained, in glowing terms, how the organization had spent seven years modernizing 370 refreshment rooms:

'The most exciting of the recent additions are the

special buffets where snacks on a grander scale are served in moderately exotic surroundings...' [It cites the Golden Arrow Bar at Victoria, the Royal Scot Bar at Euston and the Caledonia Bar at Glasgow Central as examples] 'When one compares their gay furnishings with the whistling urns and massed beer bottles of the past we seem to have come a long way.'

The late 1960s and early seventies was a period when the British pub in general also suffered a difficult time. It was the era when large numbers of historic interiors were corporately vandalised in favour of the bland, indentikit look, given meaningless names such as 'The Rat and Aardvark' and forced to serve bland keg beer epitomized by Watney's Red Barrel and Worthington 'E'. The extinction of cask-conditioned ale could not be far off. The brewers' obsession with mergers led to the creation of six big national companies, sounding the death-knell for many regional and family brewers. Companies such as Whitbread and Bass started buying out the smaller fry and their pub estates, hungry for market share. They closed regional breweries and did away with distinctive local ales. The situation was not reversed until the rise of consumer pressure, in the shape of four drinkers who decided they would fight for beer with taste and formed the Campaign for the Revitalization of Ale in 1971. That being quite a mouthful to say (especially after a few drinks) it became the Campaign for Real Ale (CAMRA), possibly the most successful consumer group ever, with a membership in 2012 of 140,000. As well as publishing the annual *Good Beer Guide* and running beer festivals, its members do important work monitoring the country's fragile stock of historic pub interiors through its Pub Heritage Group and National and Regional Inventories.

During the early CAMRA years, British Rail was a

somewhat unlikely supporter of the real ale revival when, in 1975, Travellers-Fare started replacing the fizzy keg beer with cask in the form of brews such as Draught Bass, Younger's, McEwan's and Ruddles (at 27 pence a pint), in many of its establishments. The book *Dinner in the Diner* mentions that at least one, the refreshment room at Lincoln Central, run by a 'traditionalist' manageress Miss Holt, had failed to toe the corporate line and never stopped selling it, but that's another story. Many pubs capitulated to customer demand and re-instated hand-pumps years after ripping them out, and Travellers-Fare did the same in some 40 locations. It started as a trial run at London Marylebone's Victoria & Albert Bar, which proved a success that was followed by the return of pumps at The Shires Bar at St Pancras, The Castle at Paddington, Dene's Bar at King's Cross and several station hotels. Cannon Street and Waterloo also received this treatment, along with the station pubs at Kew Gardens and Richmond.

Early in 1976 it announced its real ale revolution with a publicity campaign to spread the good news, including posters instructing drinkers to 'Make your main line station your local,' a stream of press releases and a leaflet listing outlets and supporting CAMRA. Titled *The Travellers Guide to Real Ale* and featuring bars on more than 40 stations, it bore an uncanny resemblance to the campaigners' fledgling *Good Beer Guide*. An accompanying list of brewers included long-vanished

Above: *In 1976, Travellers-Fare, part of British Rail, used this leaflet in the style of the* Good Beer Guide *to promote the reintroduction of real ale at more than 40 stations. Many continue to sell it today, though the nationalized railway system of which they were part has gone the way of keg beers such as Watney's Red Barrel and Worthington 'E'.*

The Railway at Kew Gardens is the last licensed 'on platform' pub on the London Underground. Sloane Square and Liverpool Street (Metropolitan Line) were among other examples. There is only access from the pavement now: potential customers on the platform can no longer obtain service. In the early twentieth century the station was served by steam trains of four companies, running in-between electric trains of the Metropolitan District.

beers such as Truman Tap Bitter (London), Thomas Wethered's Bitter (Marlow) and Tolly Cobbold Original (Suffolk). The London *Evening News* was exuberant:

'St Pancras Station on a wet night has traditionally fallen well behind strip clubs, night spots, theatres and bed as a source of evening entertainment. Now all that has changed... It is Real Ale that has done it... Four London station bars decided to serve proper draught beer and the hop freaks descended on them like locusts on an oasis.'

The ultimate seal of approval came in 1980 when CAMRA's Roger Protz launched that year's *Good Beer Guide* to the media and VIPs at the Victoria & Albert at Marylebone, a venue that has changed relatively little since the end of the nineteenth century.

After the liberalization of Scottish licensing law in 1976 – a precursor to all-day opening in the rest of the UK – Travellers-Fare capitalized on the new-found popularity of cocktail and lounge bars in places like Glasgow by opening two of its own. The city's Central and Queen Street Stations became locations for the incongruously-named Tropics and Berlin lounge bars – the last named reputedly with a hi-tech discotheque sound and lighting set-up built by BR's signal and telecommunications engineers. Such co-operation was indeed possible in pre-Privatization days.

By the early 1980s the 'P' word was often on the lips of politicians. British Transport Hotels was privatized in 1982-3 and the process of Travellers Fare (now without its hyphen) letting some of its small station buffets to private businesses was well underway. The station bars at Stalybridge and Manningtree, both still busy places, were early converts.

These years were also the early days of the so-called 'micro-brewery revolution', an exciting time for ale drinkers. Small, independent brewers were being set up at an increasing rate, often by experienced brewers who had been made redundant by the big companies, and were producing tasty, varied beers. (By 2010 Britain had four times as many breweries as there were at the beginning of the seventies and cask ale sales were growing, albeit from a small base compared to mass-marketed lager.) One man who knew that ideal locations for the growing choice of regional ales were on, or near, stations was a transport planner and entrepreneur, Tony Brookes. After realising the popularity of micro-brewery ales served from the cask in a chain of off-licences he started in Newcastle in 1980, the Yorkshireman had the idea to take underdeveloped spaces in stations and turn them into 'palaces of real ale'. It was not until 1994, when he walked into the former First Class Refreshment Room at Newcastle Central that the Head of Steam concept gelled:

'I knew then what I wanted to do, it was like walking into a film set, all that fabulous tile-work. I tried for two years to get a licence and spent a fortune on planning permission. But train operators weren't used to negotiating with private companies.'

Instead, his first Head of Steam opened off-station at London Euston (owned by Fuller's since 2005 and now called The Doric Arch), though another in a former booking hall in Huddersfield's magnificent station frontage quickly followed. He filled them with railway memorabilia, prints from railway artists and staged permanent beer festivals. Outlets at Scarborough and in the former North Western Hotel at Liverpool Lime Street followed. Though Brookes went on to develop licensed premises away from railways, he proved that the railway pub was a popular and viable concept in the late twentieth century.

The privatization of British Rail, which began in 1993, was a contentious issue, to say the least, and this is not the place to delve into its pros and cons. However, one side effect is that it has 'liberated' the new guardians of the nation's railway stations (namely Network Rail and individual Train Operating Companies) to continue the diversification of catering outlets that started with the selling off of British Transport Hotels in the early eighties. Small businesses are now allowed to take over often run-down units and turn some of them into attractive pubs and refreshment rooms miles away from the bland, chain outlets of earlier decades. They range from a modest micro-pub such as the Rat Race Ale House, set up in a former newsagent's on Hartlepool Station by ex-building society employee Peter Morgan; to a careful restoration of the ornate refreshment room at Sheffield Midland by a collaboration of local businessmen Jamie Hawksworth and Jon Holdsworth and Derbyshire brewer Thornbridge. In both cases, a patient lobbying of the authorities was necessary to convince them that the projects were viable and would not be swamped by rowdy 'binge drinkers' but, eventually, agreements were reached that will make other ventures easier to achieve, paving the way for attractive and varied railway pubs in the future. Mr

The Rat Race Ale House, opened on Hartlepool Station in 2009 by real ale enthusiast Peter Morgan, was the country's first 'micro-pub' on railway premises. Its diminutive size means there's no room for a counter or hand-pumps. Instead, customers are served the old-fashioned way, at their seats with beer drawn straight from the cask.

Hawksworth is also the leading light behind the reinvention of two other historic railway structures as 'craft beer houses' in 2010-11. One is the above-mentioned Edwardian tea-room on York Station; the other the Grade II listed, Portland stone gatehouses that once complemented the Euston Arch at this London terminus. That these iconic structures would be leased to a small company wanting to create speciality hostelries aimed primarily at discerning beer drinkers, would have been unthinkable in BR days. They are symbolic of how open to change Network Rail and the train operators have become.

On branch lines, the involvement of local people in the running of stations, under the aegis of Community Rail Partnerships, also bodes well. Station adoption schemes, such as that at Wemyss Bay in Scotland, where the station bar is one of several attractive features, can only help to make more stations places where people want to linger. There is no excuse for the modern railway to rest on its laurels. A need for improvements in facilities at many stations was recognised in 2006 by the All-Party Transport Select Committee. A report published three years later, by then Transport Minister Lord Adonis's 'Station Champions' Chris Green and Sir Peter Hall, condemned the dilapidated state and poor facilities at many. Manchester Victoria, Clapham Junction and Crewe were among those named 'the worst in the country'. Adonis said at the time:

> 'I want every station to be a good station – a hub of local community life and somewhere that you wouldn't mind spending time, with adequate facilities... I intend to make these minimum standards a requirement in future rail franchise agreements with train operating companies.'

The railways are a treasure-trove of historic architecture, every bit as alluring as historic houses or old churches. More than two thousand railway buildings have been listed or scheduled as being of architectural interest, a figure only exceeded by the Church of England. This is exemplified by sympathetically restored stations such as St Pancras in London and Sheffield Midland, both with pubs that have arisen from sad, run-down states.

The history of the catering industry in Britain is inextricably linked with our desire to travel and be refreshed en route. The first inns were set up at regular intervals along Roman roads. Medieval pilgrims, from Chaucer's time onwards, punctuated their journeys with regular stops for ale. Later, stage coaches clattered to a halt every 15 miles or so to change their horses and refresh their passengers at roadside inns. The warm and welcoming station pub or refreshment room was the next stage in this centuries-old story of hospitality for the traveller, and long may it continue to thrive.

3. BEER ON THE MOVE
How railways changed the brewing industry

WILLIAM HENRY WORTHINGTON, William Bass, Samuel Allsopp, James Eadie and John Marston. Just a few of the great brewers who helped make the Staffordshire town of Burton upon Trent England's undisputed 'capital of brewing'.

But this would not have been achieved without the railway. Burton's network grew into the largest private system in Europe. Never before or since have railways and breweries

enveloped a British town so comprehensively. At the peak of this rail dominance, some 20 breweries boasted their own tracks, and Burton was infused with a network of lines like a spider's web, the steel threads extending to brew houses, warehouses and ale docks, from one end of town to the other. The roads were punctuated with 32 level crossings, most equipped with their own signal box, signals and crossing gates and, for inhabitants and visitors, crossing town was sometimes akin to negotiating a vast and complex maze. People's patience was often stretched by long waits, even though trains were limited in length so that crossings were not closed to road traffic for too long. Trains of up to 50 wagons each carried the brews all over the country, travelling as far afield as London, Carlisle and Swansea direct, some carrying loads bound for the cities of the North and Scotland. Yet more was destined for export to the farthest corners of the globe.

But why did this happen in Burton of all places? Having 'the right sort of water' was a contributing factor. The most important brewing ingredient, in fact, as any beer aficionado will tell you. As far back as the seventh century, Burton's water, slowly percolated through layers of gypsum rock and drawn from wells, was regarded as having special qualities. With the reputed help of an Irish pilgrim named Modwen, miraculous cures of eye and skin ailments were even attributed to it. Four centuries later, records state that the monks of St Modwen's Abbey were brewing a superior, strong beer. Fast forward to 1708, however, and the town still only had one major brewer. It needed an efficient system of bulk transportation to distribute its superior product and this was started by water, when the Trent Navigation Act of 1712 allowed an increasing volume of beer to be shipped to the port of Hull.

The coming of the first railway in 1839, in the form of the Birmingham & Derby Junction's branch line from Hampton in

Opposite: A busy scene at Ind Coope's Burton Brewery beside the Midland Railway main line in 1894. Centre-stage is the brewery's first locomotive, an 0-4-0 well tank built circa 1863 by Thornewill & Warham, its crew exposed to the elements.

Arden, changed the mindset of the town's brewers. Then mainly small scale affairs serving local areas (like many of today's micro-breweries) they realised that the iron road would enable them to expand their distribution to far-flung places such as London and beyond, to the distant shores of the British Empire. In 1844 the Midland Railway arrived at Burton, followed in 1848 by the North Staffordshire, the LNWR in 1861 and Great Northern 1878. The industry grew in tandem: in the 1840s beer output mushroomed from 70,000 to 300,000 barrels per year; by 1870 Burton was teeming and frenetic, boasting the world's largest brewing complex, with 26 breweries. By the turn of the twentieth century it was known as a 'town of railways and beer'.

In the early days, casks were taken to the main line on floaters — four-wheeled carts each pulled by a single horse. But huge amounts of this traffic filled the streets and it became chaotic. So a logical next step was for lines to be installed into the breweries themselves. The first was constructed by the Midland for Bass in the early 1860s and it was this that evolved into Europe's pre-eminent private railway system, with 16 miles of track and running rights over a further ten of Midland lines.

The company's trains, hauled by diminutive 0-4-0 tank engines resplendent in bright red livery, with shiny brass domes, copper-capped chimneys and oversize buffers, were an impressive sight as they clanked and whistled over level crossings with strings of wagons in tow.

The company was unique in that all its traffic — supplies such as barley, malt, hops and coal and empty casks in and beer and by-products out — was handled by rail. Michael Thomas Bass (1799-1884), grandson of this company's founding brewer William, not only became a shareholder of the Midland but was keen to use the railway's services for virtually everything apart from purely local shipments. Even annual excursions for employees — the most ambitious of which was to Blackpool in 1900 when 11,241 employees travelled on 17 special trains — were by train. Under his tenure Bass became the world's largest brewer.

The distribution and receipt of huge numbers of casks, from special ale-loading stations, was run like a military campaign

Bass 0-4-0 saddle tank locomotive No.9, built in 1901 by Neilson Reid, with a saloon coach that carried King Edward VII on a tour of the company's extensive private rail network the following year. Seen at the National Brewery Centre, Burton upon Trent, beside a reconstructed ale dock where casks were manhandled on and off wagons by gangs of ale loaders.

and the system required a team of 35 clerks just to maintain the records in big ledgers. After being labelled with their destinations, thousands of heavy casks would be manhandled on to railway wagons at the ale docks, the loaded rakes then hauled by a Bass tank engine, resplendent in its 'Turkey red' livery, to the main line for marshalling into complete trains. This was done at places like Dixie exchange sidings beside the LMS line, before the engine worked to Klondyke storage sidings. The railway's board clearly had an affinity with North America when it came to naming sidings!

Traffic departments controlled the movement of railway rolling stock using their own engines and hundreds of wagons daily. The Bass system was fully signalled and even employed its own permanent way and engineering staff, with heavy overhauls carried out in dedicated locomotive shops. Horses still did some of the shunting as late as 1926. VIPs often had the honour of a ride in a four-wheeled visitors' saloon and the

size of the private network was such that a tour took more than an hour. On some days, 11 trains of 40 to 50 beer wagons each were prepared for despatch on the main line and foremost among these was the thrice-weekly 'Scotch Special' to Carlisle, connecting with trains to points north and east.

Though the largest, Bass wasn't the only railway show in town. Ind Coope, Marston, Thompson & Evershed and Truman, Hanbury and Buxton (the later with its landmark Black Eagle Brewery) all maintained their own locomotives and private sidings. The long established Worthington & Co. had a fleet of ten steam saddle tank engines as well as some petrol engine shunters, later converted to diesel.

What happened to Burton's brewery railways? By the late 1940s, road haulage was creaming off a significant share of its traffic. A national rail strike in 1955 helped to seal the system's fate. In August 1964 the last steam engine was withdrawn by Bass and, three years later, the company's rail system was silent and motionless. Let's not dwell on this sad decline however. Instead, let us turn the clock back to the early days of Britain's railway network to see what caused the brewing industry to grow in tandem.

The Liverpool & Manchester, the world's first steam hauled railway built with passengers in mind rather than solely goods, was a hit with the public as soon as it opened in 1830. With investors keen to put money into this revolutionary form of transport, Britain's basic railway network grew remarkably quickly, from 400 route miles in 1836 to more than 5,000 in the 1850s, by which time just a few sparsely populated areas, such as South West England and the Scottish Highlands, were left untouched by the iron horse. By 1870, two-thirds of the country's total network was in place. As well as providing personal mobility undreamt of by much of the population a generation earlier – from annual seaside outings to the chance to live some distance from their workplaces – it revolutionized commerce and the movement of goods. Manufactured items, merchandise, parcels and newspapers could be delivered much quicker and more reliably than before and among the sectors to benefit greatly was agriculture. Perishables such as milk, fish and meat could be sent quickly and easily to the conurbations; farmers and fishermen alike found that their produce could still be fresh and saleable when delivered to markets more than a hundred miles away.

Brewing, like farming, had catered to mainly local markets for centuries, but some canny brewers were quick to realise the effect that railway use, coupled with advertising their beer and increasing production, could have on their bottom line. One example was Kent brewer Shepherd Neame, called Shepherd and Mares in the early days. Though the company continued to use sea and road transport, in the words of the company's archivist and historian, John Owen, it also embraced the coming of the railway to dramatic effect. In 15 years it went from a small local brewery to a sizeable regional one, with distribution stores and agencies opened along the lines, hotels and pubs beside stations purchased or leased and a new malting with its own siding built at its Faversham base. Private owner wagons emblazoned with the company's name were bought and large scale advertising started for the first time. John's research, produced for the 150th anniversary of the railway coming to Faversham, explains:

'From 1858, when the railway arrived, to 1874, when output peaked, brewery production and sales increased over 300 per cent. The barrelage rose from 13,000 to 44,000 per year, the fastest rate of growth in 16 years ever.'

By 1864, when they could see the effect the new transport system had on their business, they rebuilt the brew house and modernised processes. In the following ten years output doubled.

Imagine this trend multiplied country-wide, across hundreds of breweries. The effect of small, local producers being squeezed out by so-called 'common brewers' selling on to retail vendors had started as early as the end of the sixteenth century, but the pace quickened and consumers began to drink the regional brews in ever greater quantities. The economies of large scale brewing began to kick-in, together with the development of new outlets. Among these, railway companies and brewers alike developed a new type of hotel, which sprang up beside stations large and small. The railway hotel, or rather its successor, survives in some form almost everywhere (and is probably a subject for a book of its own).

Company beer stores grew with the spreading rail routes. John Owen again:

'Some, like the London ones, were in the huge railway arches at Camberwell and Clapham... others were modest and the office at Penge, depicted in a letter of 1870, looks like something from the American 'wild west'. The stores created new employment, with little hierarchies of store keeper, clerk and draymen. The use of the horse and dray [for local deliveries] was unchanged until the widespread introduction of lorries after World War I.'

A distinctive feature of the pre-World War II railways was the variety of private owner wagons, each proclaiming the name of the coal merchant, oil company or manufacturer to which it belonged. Breweries and the malting trade contributed to this colourful collection. Shepherd Neame purchased its first wagons, from Williams and Company for use on the London, Chatham and Dover Railway, only three years after it had arrived in Faversham. By the 1870s it had about ten wagons, most sporting a smart cream livery embellished with dark blue

No.1, a private owner wagon belonging to Kent brewer Shepherd Neame, one of several that carried the company's Faversham ales to stores in South London until the 1920s.

lettering and golden yellow shading. The stylish paintwork complete with the company name in large block letters, seen by thousands as it trundled through stations and across the Kent countryside, was not just for show but played an important part in the company advertising campaign. There was a second reason that brewers employed private owner wagons, according to Ian Peaty in *Brewery Railways*. This was because wagons often spent long periods in sidings, often used as portable warehouses, and demurrage charges would have to have been paid if railway company wagons were employed. Much brewery traffic is seasonal, whether it is the delivery of hops or the shipment of larger quantities of beer to satisfy thirsty summer drinkers.

A lot of the dedicated brewery rolling stock was of the standard four-wheel van variety, but an exception was the four-wheel road-rail tank wagons, mounted on 10ft wheelbase standard steel underframes, constructed between 1939-46 and used mainly by Whitbread in an attempt to combine the bulk

There's a moose on the loose: this narrow gauge tank wagon, No.280, is used as an advertising tool by a Porthmadog brewery. It is seen at special events on the Ffestiniog and Welsh Highland Railways; here during a beer festival at Dinas in May, 2010.

advantages and speed of rail with the flexibility of road transport: the best of both worlds. A six-wheeled rail vehicle version (marked 'shunt with care' for obvious reasons) was also built by the GWR, and later used by BR Western Region, for use carrying Guinness from the company's Park Royal Brewery in North London.

What happened after the beer left the breweries by rail? Like most large brewers, Bass and Burton upon Trent's other brewers had rail depots and agents all over the country. By far the best known of these was at the Midland Railway's London St Pancras terminus. When you go to check-in for your Eurostar train to Paris or Brussels, or shop in the arcade beneath the red brick arches, you are walking in the hallowed cellars where thousands of barrels of ale were once stored. The temperature was perfect; the shipment of loaded wagons down from track level a breeze by hydraulic lift. Such was the scale of the enterprise that 120 men and 60 horses worked there continually. William Henry Barlow, who was also responsible for the magnificent, single span train-shed roof, a symphony of iron and glass, 245 feet wide, soaring 105 feet above the tracks, devised a grid of cast-iron pillars to support the tracks and platforms. These columns, 800 of them holding 2,000 wrought iron girders, were spaced using the standard beer cask as a unit of measurement. That's a little over 14 feet apart, the same as in the beer warehouses of Burton. In another architectural masterstroke, Barlow planned the horizontal girders to run the entire width of the station and double as the ties of the single-span roof — at the time of its construction the world's largest — like the strings of an upward-facing bow. For lovers of statistics, the brick arches holding up the great roof are exactly double the width of the iron columns, 29ft. 4in.: another multiple of the beer cask. So cavernous was the new vault that it required at least three fully loaded beer trains daily to keep it stocked.

The restoration of St Pancras as London's new terminal for high speed trains was completed in 2007, with the train-shed repainted in original baby blue, a replica of the giant station clock and a modern, low-roof extension for the 400 metre-long trains. It is fitting that the terminus is once again home to cask

St Pancras International in London, now the Eurostar terminus, showing a section of the former beer storage area below platform level. The supporting pillars were spaced to enable a precise number of casks to be placed between them. To the left on the upper level is a champagne bar.

Sir George Gilbert Scott's St Pancras Chambers in London, once the Midland Grand Hotel, reopened as a luxury hotel in 2011. It also houses the Betjeman Arms pub.

ale, albeit in retail rather than wholesale quantities, in the form of the Betjeman Arms. This in turn is on the site of the Shires Buffet (and the refreshment rooms run by railway caterers Spiers & Pond before that) which served generations of rail travellers. This sits in Sir George Gilbert Scott's magnificent Gothic Revival building of 1874, built sparing no expense, using Grippe's Patent Nottingham brick and several varieties of stone. It was designed so that the Midland Railway could outshine all its competitors along the Euston Road. Its public face, the Midland Grand Hotel, despite boasting sumptuously decorated public spaces, was out-of-date soon after opening. Though a first class hotel it had no central heating and, initially, only nine bathrooms (none of them en-suite). It finally closed in 1935. The former Midland Grand has, however, been re-born, reopening as luxury apartments and a five-star Marriott hotel – complete with its original interior highlight, the grand cantilevered staircase – in 2011.

What to see: Burton is still dominated by Victorian brewery buildings that contrast with the modern aluminium fermenting towers. Coopers Tavern in Cross Street, once a sampling house for the Bass brewery, is a time-warp ale house serving beers straight from the cask, while the Burton Bridge Brewery flies the flag for micro-breweries and owns five of the town's pubs. As you stroll, unmistakable brewing aromas hit you from time to time. The station was rebuilt in functional 1970s style but, nearby, the massive Midland Railway Grain Warehouse No.2, built in 1901 and now restored as offices, is a powerful reminder of the past. On the other side of the tracks is another Victorian brick behemoth, Samuel Allsopp's New Brewery (circa 1860) – the company was second only to Bass in size for much of the nineteenth century.

The National Brewery Centre (formerly the Coors Visitor Centre, Marston's Visitor Centre and Bass Museum), reopened in 2010. It tells the story of brewing in Burton from the eleventh century when Benedictine monks used the local water with reputed health-giving properties to brew a superior, strong beer. Of interest are a working stationary steam engine, vintage brewery lorries and other vehicles, as well as a large model railway depicting part of the town as it was in 1921. There is also the William Worthington micro-brewery (formerly White Shield) and exhibits telling the story of the town's railway system. There are items of rolling stock too – 0-4-0 tank locomotive Bass No.9 (built in 1901 but no longer operational), the Directors' Coach of 1889 (the saloon used for VIP railtours) and a four-wheeled diesel shunting engine No.20 – all positioned beside a reconstruction of a loading bay or 'ale dock' the like of which stood adjacent to the company's ale stores. The last named locomotive, a chain-driven 'Planet' type, is a rare survivor of a sort once common on light rail systems between World War I and II. It was delivered to Worthington & Co. Brewery in 1926.

The National Brewery Centre, Horninglow Street, Burton upon Trent, Staffordshire, DE14 1NG. Tel. 01283 532880. www.nationalbrewerycentre.co.uk

4. OFF 'OPPING
Saluting the hop-pickers

NO BOOK ON RAILWAYS, pubs and beer would be complete without paying tribute to the hop-pickers. For more than a hundred years – from the 1850s until the late 1950s – thousands of London families decamped annually to Kent on special trains for the picking season. The railways dusted off ancient passenger rolling stock and coaxed it back to life. The workforce was made up of working class folk from the East End and places such as Peckham and Rotherhithe, plus gypsies and itinerant pickers. They descended on the hop-gardens with gusto, living in temporary encampments for several weeks from late August to September, making the most of a working holiday in sylvan countryside. This migration has become part

The caption on this postcard, sent in 1905, reads 'Homeward bound. Londoners on their way to railway station.' At a place such as Paddock Wood they would have joined hundreds of other returning hoppers. Bare hop-poles decorate the background.

of the folk-lore of the East End and the Weald of Kent and was unique to its time. Thanks to farm mechanization and rising living standards, its like will never be seen again.

The hoppers were mainly women and children, though retired men often joined the throng. It was not unusual to find extended family groups of four generations travelling and working together. They regarded their trip as a summer holiday, preparing and looking forward to it for months beforehand and often returning to the same farm year after year. Hoppers' friends, including men of working age, joined their families at weekends using more special trains. The annual cycle began when prospective pickers received a postcard or letter from a farmer telling them when the crop would be ready and when to report for their train. Paddock Wood, in the heart of hop-country, was the main railhead and even boasted a 'Hop Control Room' where the dozens of trains (as many as eighty-five in 1925) could be administered. The first hoppers' specials reputedly used cattle trucks but eventually the oldest passenger stock was called into service. Fares were low, though fare-dodging was endemic, with children being disguised as babies (which were carried free), hiding under seats or the ladies' long skirts.

Trains left London Bridge (low level) very early in the morning and took slow, circuitous routes. The sight of people, many in ragged clothing and with young children clinging to them, trudging to the station through dimly-lit streets with prams full of luggage (bedclothes, pots, pans, pictures and even lace curtains) would have greeted anyone else awake in the early hours. Paddock Wood and the branch to Goudhurst and Hawkhurst were major destinations, as many as seven specials leaving London for that branch in three hours from 3.30 to 6.30 am. The sight of these long vintage trains, invariably double-headed by equally elderly engines, storming up this backwater's steep gradients (it had been engineered by the redoubtable Colonel Stephens), was a rare treat to be savoured by steam lovers. Stirling B Class 4-4-0s of the South Eastern & Chatham Railway were often the motive power in the 1920s. As a hint of things to come, the front of the very first train in 1892 was garlanded with hops, but the line closed in 1961, never having achieved the potential its founders believed it could.

Having walked or, for the lucky ones, ridden a wagon or lorry to the hop-garden, the hoppers would transform their allotted hut into a home-from-home, equipped with straw mattresses and lit by the glow of an oil-lamp. Picking started at seven each morning and long days were spent at the task, with children assisting, sustained only by a sandwich and that morning's brew of tea, decanted into bottles. The tall bines had to be pulled down first, often showering the individual with rainwater, before the tedious process of picking and filling baskets could begin. The work stained fingers and cut palms. After picking, the contents were tallied by supervisors before being emptied into hessian sacks known as 'pokes', then taken by cart to oast-houses for drying.

Normally quiet villages such as Goudhurst became bustling centres at hop-time, with thousands of high-spirited Cockneys descending on them, all intent on a good time. Jellied-eel and whelk stalls circled the village pond, crowds singing, laughing

and filling the pubs. The local hostelries, as well as butchers, bakers and grocers, could make a fortune, often working fourteen-hour days in the process. The local police were also busy – disturbances were common. Singing and dancing continued around the camp-fires, to the sound of the accordion, until late in the evening.

Return journeys to London were equally raucous and not without incident. Brian Hart, in his book *The Hawkhurst Branch*, recalls a near tragedy at Marden Station in 1895. An inebriated woman, one of a large group of returning hoppers, suddenly fell forward onto the track:

> '...a booking clerk and porter courageously leapt after her, much to the horror of the signalman who hollered at the top of his voice "Look out! The express!" Miraculously, they managed to drag her off the rails and into the six foot between the running lines as, a mere split second later, the train thundered through.'

The Rother Valley, whose steeply graded Kent & East Sussex Railway is now a heritage line, became an increasingly important hop-growing area in the early twentieth century when Arthur Guinness bought several farms at Bodiam. By the 1940s, there were more than four thousand hoppers carried each year on the K&ESR. Wagons full of pokes generated seasonal goods traffic, too, but Guinness finally sold its farms in 1976.

What to see: The K&ESR, another make-do-and-mend Colonel Stephens creation, has been preserved much as the hoppers would have known it (though the rolling stock is much better maintained). Bodiam Station, which was once surrounded by hop-gardens and where the former Guinness siding has been converted to a run-round loop, is the scene of an annual re-creation of hopping time. Held each September, it started as a reunion but has grown into a celebration of a bygone family ritual. Music and dance, a sing-song around the camp-fire and replica living huts, suitably decorated, are highlights. Visitors have a go at handling the hops, stripping them from the wiry bines. In 2008, the railway re-created the last 'Hoppers' Special' on the line, fifty years after it ran from London Bridge via Robertsbridge. The Rother Valley Brewery, adjacent to the line at Northiam, produced a limited edition Hoppers' Anniversary Ale (4.4% ABV) which they bottled for the occasion. Some of the company's ales are stocked in the railway's shop.

Hops were also grown in Herefordshire and Worcestershire, and around Alton in Hampshire, location of the Mid-Hants Steam Railway, but nowhere witnessed the late-summer flight from city to country and back on the scale seen in Kent.

Kent & East Sussex Railway, Tenterden Town Station Station Road, Tenterden, Kent, TN30 6HE. Tel. 01580 765155 www.kesr.org.uk

Opposite: *In a scene many hop-pickers would recognise, the crew of one hundred year-old 'P' class 0-6-0 tank No.753, bound for Tenterden, exchange tokens at Northiam on the Kent & East Sussex Railway in June 2010.*

Right: *Bottle label for Hoppers' Anniversary Ale, brewed in 2008 by the Rother Valley Brewery to mark the fiftieth anniversary of the last hoppers' special from London Bridge to the Kent & East Sussex Railway.*

The Kent & East Sussex Railway has been part of the rural landscape for over 100 years and carried thousands of hop pickers to the 'Guinness' hop gardens surrounding Bodiam Station. September 21st 2008 marks the 50th Anniversary of the very last such train, the "Hoppers Special" that brought hundreds of people from London Bridge Station to Robertsbridge & thence to Bodiam for the adjoining hop gardens.
In commemoration of this historic event, the Rother Valley Brewery, in association with the K&ESR, have produced this limited edition Hoppers Anniversary Ale.

HOPPERS ANNIVERSARY ALE

Rother Valley Brewing Company was established in Northiam in 1993 on a hop farm overlooking the River Rother that marks the boundary between Kent & East Sussex.
Traditional Sussex hops have been grown on the farm adjacent to our brewery for over 200 years and the family who have farmed this land for nearly a century have maintained the tradition and grown all the hops used in this brew.
Rother Valley Brewing Company brew cask ales and bottled beers for distribution to many public houses and shops in Kent and East Sussex.

ABV 4.4%   500ml

HAND BREWED ALE

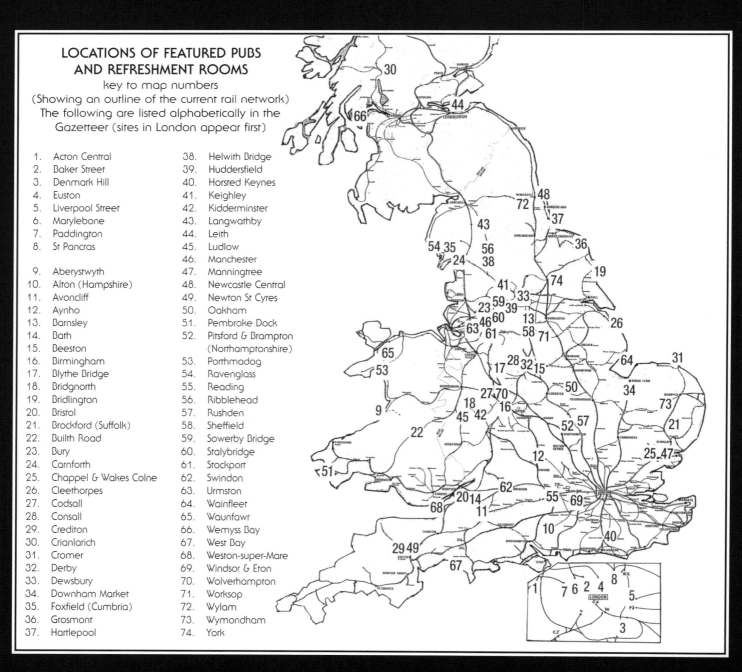

LOCATIONS OF FEATURED PUBS AND REFRESHMENT ROOMS
key to map numbers
(Showing an outline of the current rail network)
The following are listed alphabetically in the Gazetteer (sites in London appear first)

1. Acton Central
2. Baker Street
3. Denmark Hill
4. Euston
5. Liverpool Street
6. Marylebone
7. Paddington
8. St Pancras

9. Aberystwyth
10. Alton (Hampshire)
11. Avoncliff
12. Aynho
13. Barnsley
14. Bath
15. Beeston
16. Birmingham
17. Blythe Bridge
18. Bridgnorth
19. Bridlington
20. Bristol
21. Brockford (Suffolk)
22. Builth Road
23. Bury
24. Carnforth
25. Chappel & Wakes Colne
26. Cleethorpes
27. Codsall
28. Consall
29. Crediton
30. Crianlarich
31. Cromer
32. Derby
33. Dewsbury
34. Downham Market
35. Foxfield (Cumbria)
36. Grosmont
37. Hartlepool

38. Helwith Bridge
39. Huddersfield
40. Horsted Keynes
41. Keighley
42. Kidderminster
43. Langwathby
44. Leith
45. Ludlow
46. Manchester
47. Manningtree
48. Newcastle Central
49. Newton St Cyres
50. Oakham
51. Pembroke Dock
52. Pitsford & Brampton (Northamptonshire)
53. Porthmadog
54. Ravenglass
55. Reading
56. Ribblehead
57. Rushden
58. Sheffield
59. Sowerby Bridge
60. Stalybridge
61. Stockport
62. Swindon
63. Urmston
64. Wainfleet
65. Waunfawr
66. Wemyss Bay
67. West Bay
68. Weston-super-Mare
69. Windsor & Eton
70. Wolverhampton
71. Worksop
72. Wylam
73. Wymondham
74. York

5. GAZETTEER

As it is the hub of the railway system, entries in Greater London are given first,
followed by those in the rest of England, Scotland and Wales

THE FOLLOWING PAGES contain a personal selection of historical, ornate or quirky railway-orientated places of refreshment you can visit. It is not intended to be a comprehensive survey: such a directory would be a weighty tome indeed. I have concentrated on establishments occupying original railway buildings. Those not so located have some other association which is explained in the text. A bias towards places on lines that are open and in regular operation is intentional: the best way to visit railway pubs is by train, though all can, of course, be reached by car as well. (I was often able to make considerable savings by using advance purchase and rover tickets.)

The descriptions are based partly on personal observation and, though I have attempted to be as objective as possible, they may differ from readers' impressions and are subject to human error, for which I apologize in advance. With one or two exceptions, restaurants and hotels have been excluded as they are specialist areas deserving of separate study. Changes and suggestions for future editions are welcome at bartonwrite1@gmail.com. Regular updates will be posted on www.facebook.com/railwaypubs.

NOTES

Unless stated otherwise, all establishments are licensed to sell alcohol and serve cask conditioned beer, referred to as 'real ale'. When early morning opening hours are given, licensed alcohol sales may not start until later. When railway memorabilia is mentioned in descriptions, some artefacts may be reproductions rather than originals.

All information is given purely for guidance and may change at short notice. Readers are advised to check opening times before travelling.

The entries should not be considered recommendations in terms of drink, cuisine or service, the quality of which can be transient. Establishments stand on their own merit and none have paid nor provided other inducements to be included.

'CAMRA' refers to the Campaign for Real Ale, an independent, consumer-run organization, founded in 1971 and committed to supporting Britain's unique beer style and pubs. For more details visit www.camra.org.uk, tel. 01727 867201.

LONDON – ACTON CENTRAL

Former North London Railway
(now London Overground) between
Willesden Junction and Richmond.

THE STATION HOUSE

The capital has no less than seven stations with Acton in their title, including East, West, North and South, and four of them are on the Underground network. This one was opened in 1853 as, simply, 'Acton' by the North & South Western Junction Railway – the 'Central' was appended later – and it was served by trains of the North London Railway. Next to a busy level crossing and occupying the larger part of a handsome station building, including the former booking hall, it is now a contemporary bar.

With its canopy sheltering drinkers at tables on the cobbled former driveway, the building's exterior is well preserved. No interior railway era fittings remain but this is a rare station building where customers are able to ascend to the upper floor, now called the Rosso Room. Its open roof space, revealing the original matrix of heavy wooden truss-beams and wall brackets and large round-headed windows overlooking the station, is rather splendid. The room opens in the evenings and

Sunday afternoons, though may be accessible at other times. An open kitchen and small bar counter is accommodated here. The downstairs room is also open-plan and has the main bar counter. There is usually at least one real ale – Sharp's Doom Bar on my visit, plus some Belgian bottled beers. A menu, including pizza and 'southern Italian tapas', is served all day. An unusual feature on the station is a sign advising drivers of electric units to switch from overhead 25Kv AC to DC third-rail pick-up. Diesel-hauled freights also pass through: this strategic cross-London route connects with various main lines radiating from the metropolis.

Nearby: Several of television's *Monty Python* comedy sketches were shot on this road and the team's 'Hell's Grannies' skit on Acton High Street.

The Station House, 12 Station Buildings, Churchfield Road, Acton, London W3 6BH. Tel. 0208 992 7110. Daily from noon until midnight (Friday, Saturday, 1am), Sunday, Monday, 11pm. www.thestationhousew3.com

LONDON – BAKER STREET

Former Metropolitan Railway between Paddington and Farringdon and Finchley Road and other London Underground lines.

THE METROPOLITAN BAR

Once the Metropolitan Railway's plush, 250-cover Chiltern Court Restaurant, opened in 1929, now an emporium of the J.D. Wetherspoon pub chain. In the words of the late poet laureate Sir John Betjeman, this was

'...Where the wives of Pinner and Ruislip would sit after a day's shopping... awaiting their husbands coming up from Cheapside and Mincing Lane... listening to the band playing for the *thé dansant...*'

Notable male customers included H.G. Wells and Arnold Bennett. The embodiment of the ideals of Metro-land, this was an oasis perched above the most important station on the company's system – the world's first underground railway – a stone's throw from Sherlock Holmes's residence! It is part of the Chiltern Court building, a nine storey block of flats in Portland stone by the MR's architect C.W. Clark, begun in 1911 and completed in 1930, a section of which was used for briefing Special Operations Executive (SOE) agents in World War II.

The pearl-clad ladies who lunched have been replaced by groups of casually dressed folk, often 'escapees' from Madame Tussaud's and other tourists, but elegance survives. Entrance is almost theatrical. Climbing steps, one turns to see a cavernous auditorium, softly lit by uplighters, its ceiling supported by seven classical-style columns and decorated with painted plaster mouldings. The ceiling is divided into squares, each set with four coats-of-arms, including that of the Metropolitan Railway and some of the places it served. A counter now stretches along half of one wall and 18 hand-pumps were serving eight cask ales. Meals (including breakfast) are available from opening time until late evening.

Nearby: The station's sub-surface platforms, built using the cut-and-cover method, opened in 1863 and were restored in 1983 to their Victorian look. Near the Marylebone Road entrance is a statue of fictional detective Sherlock Holmes. A plaque locates his supposed home, 221B Baker Street.

The Metropolitan Bar, 7 Station Approach, Marylebone Road, London, NW1 5LA. Tel. 0207 486 3489. Monday to Saturday 8am – 11.30pm, Sunday 10am – 11pm. www.jdwetherspoon.co.uk

Below left: *The Chiltern Court development was served by its own siding, used by coal and rubbish trains, at Baker Street. Metropolitan 1921 electric locomotive No.7,* Edmund Burke, *completes the final delivery of coal on 3 August, 1961.* Below right: *The Metropolitan Bar, formerly the Chiltern Court Restaurant.*

LONDON – DENMARK HILL

Former London, Brighton & South Coast Railway. Now served by London Overground trains and others from London Victoria, London Bridge, Blackfriars, Sevenoaks, Dartford and other destinations.

THE PHOENIX

When a fire tore through this station in 1980 it seemed like the end for another piece of railway heritage: the Italianate station building, with its French convex roofs, dates from 1865. Instead, from the ashes arose a Civic Trust Award-winning (1985) restoration and a brewpub in the lofty entrance hall. Both the home brewing aspect, in the aptly named Phoenix and Firkin, and David Bruce's Firkin Brewery chain of which it was part, have gone (from the UK at least). After a spell as O'Neill's it changed hands again and was given its current name. The handsome, symmetrical building is of yellow brick, with semi-circular door and window arches. Cast-iron, decorative roof-railings run between the two wings.

The large bar is set in the centre of the station building, which is on a road bridge above the four platforms and tracks. It has been left open up to the joists, giving a feeling of space. A large railway clock, by Potts & Co. of Leeds, is a focal point. Time stands still here as the hands no longer move! Bare brickwork, wood floors and a brick fireplace create a rustic feel. There are sofas with deep cushions and a leather banquette. A spiral staircase climbs to mezzanine level, overlooking the platforms. The entrance is adjacent to that of the current booking hall. There are doors (not in general use) onto the station's glazed, veranda-style footbridge. On my visit, all four hand-pumps were in use, dispensing Sambrook's Junction, Fuller's London Pride, Sharp's Doom Bar and Wells' Bombardier. Real cider and bottled beers including Duvel and Sierra Nevada were available. Wide menu served all day until late; Sunday roasts. Children welcome.

The station: Canopies remain on all four platforms and they

The Phoenix.

Denmark Hill Station was restored as a pub after a fire in 1980.

are supported by slim iron columns with delicate decoration and brackets. There are 'candy-twist' lamp standards.

The Phoenix, Denmark Hill Station, Windsor Walk, London SE5 8BB. Tel. 0207 703 8767. Daily noon – 11pm (Friday, Saturday, midnight, Sunday 10.30pm). www.thephoenixwindsorwalk.co.uk

LONDON – EUSTON

Former London & Birmingham Railway
(later LNWR), terminus of the West Coast main line to
Liverpool, Manchester and Glasgow
(also London Underground).

THE EUSTON TAP & CIDER TAP

A pair of Portland stone entrance lodges that once flanked the avenue leading to the iconic Euston Arch (demolished in 1961/62) have new uses as speciality beer and cider houses. The western structure became, in 2010, the setting for what was claimed to be the capital's first 'craft beer house'. Eight cask micro-brewery ales are served, across a range of styles, plus a large selection of craft beers, both keg and bottled, foreign and domestic. The two storey, Grade II listed Romanesque structures, designed by J.B. Stansby in 1869, have few windows and one pair of doors each. They bear LNWR monograms carved along with the names of places served by its trains or those of its allies. Inside

Entrance to Euston Station, London.

The Euston Tap and Cider Tap are situated behind the artist who drew this LNWR postcard image of the Euston Arch.

the beer house, a square, quarry-tiled room is dominated by a three-sided bar counter devoid of hand-pumps. Replica 1904 Czech beer taps, set on the bar-back, do the job instead: ale is supplied from the cellar casks by 'air-driven cylinder'. Above them a row of 19 American-style taps dispense speciality world beers, complemented by an eye-catching variety of bottled beers from several countries (especially Germany and the USA) displayed in two wardrobe-size cool cabinets.

Limited seating is on bar-stools: a cast-iron spiral staircase winds to an upper room where there's a greater seating capacity, mainly on leather upholstered benches. Decoration includes copies of architects' drawings of the Euston Arch and its associated buildings, from the National Archives. The ever changing beer list is marked up on blackboards – including examples from Brewdog, Bristol Beer Factory, Thornbridge, Marble and Fyne Ales – all hard to find elsewhere in London. No meals are served but there is a pizza ordering service in the evenings. The size and popularity of the hostelry contributes to its atmosphere (there is also background music) and it can quickly become crowded. There are limited toilet facilities,

Travellers approaching the Euston Arch first passed this stone lodge, one of a pair on the Euston Road, now home to a craft beer house.

A late 19th century advertisement shows the West Lodge once contained a ticket agent for Guion Line steamships plying between Liverpool and New York.

reached by a steep staircase and outside seating.

The eastern lodge opened as the Cider Tap in late 2011. At least eight draught and still ciders and perries are served, the 'menu' being shown on a blackboard. An underground passage, once used as a subterranean shooting gallery, links the two buildings but is no longer open.

The 72ft-high, Greek Revival style gateway known as the Euston Arch, designed by Philip Hardwick, once formed a triumphant entrance to London's first main line terminus. If the Euston Arch Trust, whose patron is writer and broadcaster Michael Palin, has its way, this edifice will be re-built as part of the station's proposed re-development as the terminus of High Speed Two. Its cast-iron gates, complete with insignia of the London & Birmingham Railway, are preserved at the National Railway Museum, York.

Nearby: Real ale enthusiasts are spoilt for choice. Between the Euston Tap and the station is The Doric Arch, a Fuller's house with an array of railway memorabilia and a liberal guest beer selection. The Bree Louise, two minutes west of the station in Coburg Street, serves up to 19 ales, many straight from the cask.

The Euston Tap, West Lodge, 190 Euston Road, London NW1 2EF. Tel. 0203 137 8837.
Monday to Saturday, Noon – 11.30pm, Sunday 2 – 10pm.
Cider Tap, daily 3 – 11.30pm (Sunday 10pm).
www.eustontap.com

LONDON – LIVERPOOL STREET

Terminus of the former Great Eastern Railway serving destinations in eastern England
(also London Underground).

HAMILTON HALL

It is quite a surprise to step from a frenetic terminus (albeit one sensitively restored in the early 1990s) into this stately hall, lavishly decorated in Rococo style, complete with 'classical oil paintings', a marble fireplace and candelabras. Despite appearances, Hamilton Hall is not an eighteenth century creation but of the early twentieth; and is not part of the station but was once the ballroom of the former Great Eastern Hotel, extended in 1901 and whose main entrance is on Liverpool Street. It is named after Lord Claud Hamilton, chairman and long-time board member of the Great Eastern Railway, who would no doubt be taken aback to hear it is a public house.

The mezzanine is reached via a curving staircase with delicate balusters cast with swirling leaves and grapes. These are set with plaster bas-reliefs of reclining females. There are mirrors aplenty, many topped with GER monograms, and natural light floods in on one side. Ten hand-pumps on the curving lower counter serve a wide range of cask ales (and five on a smaller one upstairs). Visited by football fans on match days, sometimes the place can be crowded. Meals served all day (including breakfast). Children upstairs; outdoor drinking area; train departure screens.

The station: The 75ft.-high, four span train-shed was designed by GER engineer Edward Wilson in 1875, a delicate tracery of wrought iron and glass resembling Gothic cathedral vaulting. The walkway above the main concourse, created in the 1990s remodelling, reveals other details, including the GER Great War Memorial and moulded brick features such as a locomotive, steamship and a fireman. Outside the Liverpool Street entrance is a statue dedicated to the Jewish Children of the Kindertransport.

Hamilton Hall, Street-level Concourse (Bishopsgate entrance), Liverpool Street Station, City of London, EC2M 7PY. Tel. 0207 247 3579. Monday to Saturday 7am – 11.30pm, Sunday 9am – 11.30pm. www.jdwetherspoon.co.uk

Hamilton Hall.

LONDON - MARYLEBONE

Terminus of the former Great Central Railway, now with services to Aylesbury, Stratford-upon-Avon, Birmingham and beyond (also London Underground).

THE VICTORIA & ALBERT

This refreshment room, on the concourse of one of London's smallest termini, contains reminders of the much loved Great Central. Though restored in 1971 it is little changed, consisting of two dark wood panelled rooms. Original decorative plasterwork shines below the high ceilings. There is a wood and marble fire surround and stained glass in the round-headed windows of the former dining room. The number of hand-pumps indicate that the turnover of cask ale used to be voluminous; on my last visit there were four examples, including Fuller's London Pride, Greene King St Edmunds and Old Speckled Hen. After many years in the doldrums, at one time coming close to closure, Marylebone's fortunes have been revived. The V&A remains an oasis of calm by comparison, despite its background music and there are 'outside' tables on a busy concourse.

Food is served all day; train departure screens; toilets. Children welcome.

The station: There are GCR monograms in the railings and gates; the original booking hall, with its wood-panelled ticket windows, is now a food store. A plaque marks the centenary of poet Sir John Betjeman who loved this place. An exhibition about the station's history fills the western entrance, informing that it was the last of the capital's main line termini to open, in 1899, and is among the least altered. It doesn't mention the crowds that gathered in 1964 when The Beatles filmed scenes here for *A Hard Day's Night*. A *port cochère* (vehicle porch) links the red brick frontage with the former Great Central Hotel, previously headquarters of the British Railways Board and now a hotel once again, the Landmark London.

The Victoria & Albert, Marylebone Station, Melcombe Place, London, NW1 6JR. Tel. 0207 402 0676. Monday to Friday 11am – 11pm, Saturday 10am – 10pm, Sunday 10am – 8pm.

The bar at Marylebone, with its mahogany fittings and decorative plasterwork, has changed little since opening in 1899.

LONDON – PADDINGTON

Terminus of the former Great Western Railway to Bristol and other destinations (also London Underground).

THE MAD BISHOP & BEAR

Half hidden in former GWR offices high above the concourse, this is a tied house (rare for a London terminus) belonging to London's oldest independent brewer, Fuller's. Opened in 1999 as part of a redevelopment of the concourse, known as the 'Lawn', by architect Nicholas Grimshaw, its unusual name was chosen from entries for a brewery-run competition. The 'mad bishop' is whichever one authorised the sale of many acres of church land, at low cost, to the GWR for its new terminus! The bear is the Paddington from children's literature who was discovered at the station en route from 'Darkest Peru'. His statue can be seen below, set incongruously between Yo! Sushi and Krispy Kreme doughnuts. Wall decoration includes sepia photographs of the 1890s' station, and the 300ft-high Great Wheel that stood trackside at Earl's Court from 1895, preceding the London Eye by a century. Until a recent redecoration, reaching the toilets entailed walking a corridor lined with prints from oil paintings of old London scenes. It had the feel of a forgotten corner of the GWR: I almost expected to be passed by a 1930s' GWR clerk rushing along with a sheaf of telegraph messages. This area was once part of the company's Departure Side office extension, built *circa* 1933.

The split-level interior has a chandelier and mirrors (not original) and a marble-topped bar with nine hand-pumps. There's a good variety of Fuller's beers and a guest (St Austell Tribute on my visit). Breakfast is served from opening time with the main menu from 11am until late. 'Outdoor' area beneath roof canopy. Ambient music, train information. Children welcome.

The station: Built by Isambard Kingdom Brunel and Sir Matthew Digby Wyatt in 1854, highlights include the original three-span train-shed roof, inspired by the Crystal Palace; iron-framed oriel windows with balconies at the transepts; a statue of Brunel; and the Great Western Royal Hotel, the country's largest when opened by Prince Albert, now the Hilton Paddington.

Mad Bishop & Bear, First Floor, The Lawn, Paddington Station, London, W2 1HB. Tel. 0207 402 2441. Monday to Saturday 8am – 11pm (Friday 11.30pm), Sunday 10am – 10.30pm. www.fullers.co.uk

Top right: *The Mad Bishop & Bear.*

Lower right: *The GWR's Quick Lunch & Snack Bar, seen here in 1936, was a popular Art Deco addition to Paddington but in a different location to the Mad Bishop.*

LONDON - ST. PANCRAS INTERNATIONAL

Terminus of High Speed One to East Kent, the Continent via the Channel Tunnel, and the former Midland Railway main line to Derby and beyond. Stations for Thameslink (Bedford to Brighton) and London Underground.

THE BETJEMAN ARMS

Advertising itself as 'the last pub before Paris' – and one that combines a genuine interest in real ale accompanying good food – this is part of the architectural feast that is one of the world's great railway termini. Opened in 2008, the Betjeman occupies a corner of St Pancras Chambers, the extravagant Victorian Gothic building for the Midland Railway by Sir George Gilbert Scott. Incorporating the bar area that, in BR days, was The Shires, there are three large rooms, and two outside terraces. One of these overlooks Euston Road and at the other (with its

The dining room of the Betjeman Arms includes a corner dedicated to the late poet laureate who helped rescue St Pancras Station in the sixties.

Below: St Pancras in 'pre-Eurostar' days: a 'Peak' leaves with the 2.05pm to Nottingham and a gang of platelayers work on the track, on 28 April, 1972.

own bar counter) you can sit beneath William Henry Barlow's magnificent station roof, with a view of the Eurostar trains. Decoration is contemporary, the spaces filled with light from the Gothic windows. One room contains a marble fireplace, eclectic items of furniture and a spot I call 'Betjeman corner'. It is a collection of photographs and books relating to the late poet laureate, after whom the pub is named and whose campaigning helped save the building from demolition in the 1960s. There is a statue of him on the upper concourse.

The house beer, Betjeman Ale (brewed in Cornwall by Sharp's) was joined by guest ales Sambrook's Junction and Rooster's Celtic Corker on my visit. Festivals are held occasionally, when some beers are served straight from the cask at the concourse bar. Meals (including breakfast) from a wide ranging menu are served until 9.30pm. Train departure screens; toilets.

The station: see pages 32–34.

> **The Betjeman Arms, Unit 53, St Pancras International, Pancras Road, London, N1C 4QL. Tel. 0207 923 5440. Daily 9am – 11pm. www.geronimo-inns.co.uk/thebetjemanarms**

ABERYSTWYTH, CEREDIGION

Former Cambrian Railways (later GWR) terminus of lines from Shrewsbury and Devil's Bridge (the latter narrow gauge, now a heritage railway).

YR HEN ORSAF

What better way to start, or complete a journey on one of Wales' most scenic narrow gauge steam railways than with a drink in a former GWR station of 1924? Here, the locos of the Vale of Rheidol line complete their run of more than 11 miles from Devil's Bridge. The Edwardian-Georgian station frontage, in white stone, looks important but is fairly plain. At one end is a clock turret that seems unfinished, though the clock was restored

Yr Hen Orsaf.

in 2011. Behind is an attractive, glazed station canopy (part of which shelters outdoor diners). Above the one platform that remains in use for main line trains is a lean-to glazed awning with ornate iron columns and trusses. This adjoins a red brick Cambrian Railways building with stone arches, some inlaid with quatrefoil decoration picked out in red, green and white. The main building, Grade II listed, was converted by the J.D. Wetherspoon pub chain in 2002 at a cost of £1.2 million. It won a National Rail Heritage Award in 2003.

Yr Hen Orsaf is Welsh for 'the old station' and the pub is frequented by tourists as well as locals. One jokingly asked if I was 'Dai the Spy' as he spotted me writing notes. He pointed out areas that were the original refreshment room and booking office (the ticket windows are still in place). A separate restaurant across the concourse was previously the parcels and left luggage offices. Another of the pub's customers has gone down in local folklore. He came in one morning in June 2006, had a couple of pints and put 'as much as £10,000' in cash on the table (according to the *Guardian* newspaper, 22 June 2006,

G2, page 2). After drinking he went outside and threw the money up in the air with the rallying call 'Who wants free money?', to the delight of passers-by. Neither his identity nor motive were reported. The large pub has several seating areas but just one bar counter, with ten hand-pumps. Regular ales like Marston's Pedigree are complemented by guests such as Woods of Shropshire and York Brewery, plus ciders. Meals, served all day (including breakfast), is usual Wetherspoon's fare with some Welsh specialities. Décor and furnishings are functional but sympathetic with the 1920s era; in one section original paving has been retained.

Nearby: This Victorian seaside resort includes a pier, graceful, curving promenade and Britain's longest electric cliff railway, climbing Constitution Hill, atop which is a *camera obscura*.

Yr Hen Orsaf, Aberystwyth Station, Alexandra Road,
Aberystwyth, SY23 1LN. Tel. 01970 636080.
Daily 7am – midnight (Fri./Sat. 1am).
www.jdwetherspoon.co.uk

ALTON, HAMPSHIRE

Current termini of the former London & South Western Railway from London (Waterloo) and the Mid-Hants Railway (a heritage line).

THE REAL ALE TRAIN (RAT)

It wasn't that long ago that a train full of 300 people drinking large quantities of beer and making merry would have drawn forth van loads of police officers and tabloid headlines containing words such as 'yob' and 'mindless'. The fact that the Mid-Hants 'Watercress Line' can fill some 24 trains a year with polite and good-humoured people, who enjoy the combination of real ale and steam, is a tribute to ale drinkers in general and the volunteers who run the railway in particular.

By 7.20pm, when West Country class 4-6-2 number 34007

The Real Ale Train is usually a sell-out. This is the busy bar car on March 27, 2010, when West Country class No.34007 Wadebridge *was the motive power.*

Wadebridge is easing the RAT out of Alton station, my friend Richard and I have found seats, purchased our first pint and are alternately taking a sip of beer and breath of steam from the open window. Every seat on the train is taken and the mood of our fellow travellers is 'kid in candy store'. There is free movement along the gangways towards the nerve-centre. This is the bar car, a Mark I British Railways mail carriage converted to contain a long bar top, six large casks sunk neatly into it. Volunteers in black t-shirts work feverishly to supply passengers with beer, at a nostalgic price of £2 per pint. Each train focuses on the produce of two independent breweries. Tonight there are five ales, from Triple fff (brewed near the line) and Dark Star from West Sussex; and a cider, Newton's Discovery. The train also contains a Mark I Griddle Car with its informal seating arrangement, and a counter, where the catering crew is serving curry, including a vegetarian option, from large vats.

Part of the fun is that most, sometimes all, the journey is done after dark. One can slide open a window and see, in the moonlight, a red-hot glow around the footplate and sparks flying out of the loco's chimney as she powers up the gradient –

among the steepest in England. At a midway station we raise our (plastic) glasses to passengers passing on the *Watercress Belle*, a dining train. At Alresford, end of the ten-mile line, we stroll a platform lit with gas lamps, glowing semaphore signal lamps and, inside the immaculate station, a blazing coal fire.

The Mid-Hants Railway survived the Beeching cuts of the 1960s only to be closed by British Railways in 1973. Four years later it was taken over by enthusiasts running steam instead of diesel. Its nick-name, the Watercress Line, comes from the large quantities of the produce it carried. It could easily have been the Hop Garden Line, for this was once prime hop-growing territory. In the 1860s, Crowley's Alton ales were popular as far away as London. Back on our train, we are making our second and last return to Alton, where we need only cross a footbridge to catch a main-line train back to London (after two round trips, the train connects with a South West Trains departure to the capital). The bar staff are patiently coaxing the last pints from the barrels with the revelation: 'You lot have drunk us dry tonight!'

Nearby: Alton is an attractive market town and two minutes' walk from the station, in Anstey Road, is the Railway Arms (tel. 01420 82218). It is easy to spot as a miniature Southern Railway steam engine is emerging from the wall. Owned by the Triple fff Brewery, it serves the full range, including Alton's Pride, CAMRA's Champion Beer of Britain 2008, as well as micro-brewery guests. With its horseshoe bar and high-back pews, it's busy and full of character. Chawton, two miles away, was home to novelist Jane Austen and her cottage is open to visitors.

> **The Real Ale Train departs on Saturday evenings, one to three times a month (February to December) from Alton Station, Hampshire, GU34 2PZ. Prior booking is essential, tel. 01962 733810. www.watercressline.co.uk**

With a train full of happy drinkers, the 'RAT' steams between Ropley and Medstead, with BR 5MT No.73096 in charge, in September 2008.

AVONCLIFF, WILTSHIRE

Former Great Western Railway between
Bath Spa and Trowbridge.

THE CROSS GUNS

From the garden at the Cross Guns you can gaze across the River Avon and see two important transport routes squeezed together at the valley's narrowest point. The older one is the Kennet & Avon Canal, an eighteenth century engineering marvel, using lock flights and stone aqueducts to link the rivers Thames and Avon. The other is the former Great Western Railway, whose (initially broad gauge) steam chariots swept down the Limpley Stoke Valley at breakneck speed and quickly killed the canal's business. I chose neither, instead taking my folding Brompton bicycle on a High Speed Train (HST) to Bath, cycling along the towpath from there. For those arriving

The Cross Guns.

at Avoncliff by train, the pub is less than three minutes' stroll, over an aqueduct. Being a request stop, passengers must advise the train manager if they wish to alight and, when boarding, give a hand signal.

With sections dating from the fifteenth to the seventeenth centuries, this former drovers' inn of Cotswold stone is not a railway building but has served as a watering-hole for railway builders and travellers alike, as it did for the canal navvies before them. It features an inglenook fireplace similar to those at Hampton Court Palace; a priest's hiding hole (complete with table and chairs for reclusive drinkers) and an oak-beamed ceiling. It is one of two brewery taps for the Box Steam Brewery, the 'Great Western Ale', whose beers include Tunnel Vision and the summer special, Golden Bolt, previously called Rev. Awdry after the author of *Thomas the Tank Engine* stories. Ken Roberts, proprietor of the Cross Guns, liked the beer so much he took over the brewery. Complementing three Box Steam ales, the compact bar offered two guests, Northumberland Ale and Theakston's Old Peculier; also there are fruit wines and malt whiskies. A wide menu is served daily at lunchtime and in the evening. Children and dogs are welcome and accommodation available. A terraced garden slopes towards the river, shaded with willows and conifers; there's the sound of water tumbling over a nearby weir. The location is, however, not ideal for the mobility impaired arriving by train due to steps up from the station.

Nearby: The railway goes through lovely countryside and closely follows the Kennet & Avon Canal, which it crosses beneath Dundas Aqueduct. North of Avoncliff is a disused but intact station at Limpley Stoke and beyond there, the junction with the closed Camerton branch, where the 1953 Ealing comedy *The Titfield Thunderbolt* was filmed.

The Cross Guns, Avoncliff, near Bradford on Avon, Wiltshire, BA15 2HB. Tel. 01225 862335/867613. Daily 10am – midnight (Friday and Saturday 1am). www.crossguns.net

AYNHO, OXFORDSHIRE (station closed)

Former Great Western Railway between Oxford and Banbury.

GREAT WESTERN ARMS

An inn sign bearing the Great Western Railway's coat-of-arms, topped with a semaphore signal arm, hints to the railway delights to be found within this hostelry. Set on the border with Northamptonshire between a wharf on the Oxford Canal and long-closed Aynho station on the lower of two busy rail routes, is this creeper-clad pub. Justly popular for its food and ale, diners are advised to book. Though not a railway building – there has been a pub on this site since the coming of the canal – it was extended and altered to cope with extra business generated by the railway's arrival. Several rooms, with candle-lit tables and floors variously of flagstones, quarry tiles and wood, are grouped around a stone-built, open hearth fire and wood-panelled bar. The latter features a GWR wall clock. The railway-oriented decoration is mainly of Great Western origin, some local to the area. There are prints, photographs, tickets, cast-iron wagon plates and 'no trespass' signs, a GW period route map and boundary marker of 1889, and posters for livestock auctions held at the station in the early twentieth century.

Beer is from the local Hook Norton brewery (Ali's Ale and Old Hooky are regulars, joined by a seasonal special). A courtyard garden leads to a barn containing a traditional long-alley skittle game. A wide menu is served at most times, though not between 3-6pm (when sandwiches may be available). Children and dogs are welcome. Background music; overnight accommodation.

The adjacent station building is a standard single-storey Brunel design in local stone, built in 1850 and now a private house. Its distinctive, all-round awning has been reduced but does have realistic valancing. Peculiar lion's head masks of cast-iron once decorated this at intervals on the outward-facing sides (as they did at some other stations) but these have been

The Great Western Arms: the station building is hidden behind trees.

removed. The Oxford-bound platform is overgrown and its buildings demolished (the last passengers left in 1964) though the line is kept busy with passenger and freight traffic. In the distance is a girder bridge carrying the line from High Wycombe and Bicester towards the point where both routes meet at Aynho Junction. This 'high line' formed part of the GWR's direct London – Birmingham route, the last main line railway built in England until HS1 this century. Its station in the vicinity was Aynho Park, in use for more than 50 years, until 1963. The most appealing way to arrive today is by canal boat; or walking the towing path, though parking is available for motorists.

Nearby: Those with their own transport might like to visit the Hook Norton Brewery (ten miles west in Hook Norton), an excellent example of a Victorian tower brewery, complete with a working steam engine. There is a visitor centre and tours (tel. 01608 730384).

Great Western Arms, Aynho Wharf, Station Road (off B4031) near Banbury, Oxfordshire, OX17 3BP. Tel. 01869 338288. Daily 11am – 11pm. Nearest station: Kings Sutton (less than four miles). www.hooky-pubs.co.uk

BARNSLEY (COURT HOUSE), SOUTH YORKSHIRE (station closed)

Former Midland Railway between Court House Junction and Sheffield or Cudworth.

THE COURTHOUSE

This building has a chequered history, being built as a court house in 1861, bought by the Midland for use as a station in 1870 and becoming a pub shortly after the line's closure in 1960. A royal coat-of-arms resides over the main entrance as a reminder of its original role. The Venetian architectural style, in ashlar stone, is a dramatic contrast to the stark, modern lines of Bradford Interchange rail and bus station, situated opposite.

The large U-shaped bar room, with its central counter, raised dining area and bench-lined 'snugs' in two corners, gives few clues to its former use, though ale drinkers will, in any case, be distracted by the three hand-pumps, two of which were dispensing beers by highly regarded Barnsley brewer Acorn (Darkness and Top Station on my visit). 'Top station' was local

Barnsley Court House on September 14, 1959 showing Robinson C13 class 4-4-2 No.67445. The station building, now the pub, is below platform level.

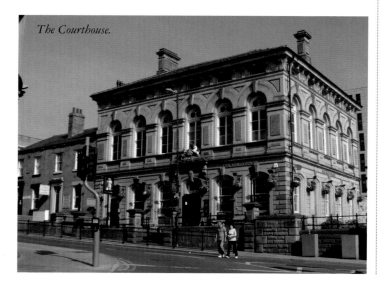

The Courthouse.

parlance for this station, the reason being clear if you climb the multi-level staircase from the twin-arched stairwell to the landing, where Midland Railway style trefoil windows (repeated on the outer first floor windows) are a prominent feature of the upper doorway. The platforms were at this upper level, the railway crossing town on a viaduct, so intending passengers had to ascend from the booking hall where the bar is now situated. Among local historical photographs (and local art prints) to be seen are some of the station in steam days, along with a coal fire, and wall panelling which may date from the railway era. Pub fare is served all day, starting with breakfast and there are Sunday roasts. There is a paved outdoor drinking area at the front. Background music, games machines, pool table.

Howard Needham, a friend who grew up in the town, remembers an ill-fated Sunday morning children's excursion to Blackpool from the station as a boy in the mid 1950s:

'There were hundreds of children and mothers on the elevated platform. On the train we were all given packed lunches containing potted meat sandwiches, a bag of crisps with salt wrapped in blue paper, some fruit and a bottle of Vimto. It was a glorious day, but on the return journey the locomotive broke down somewhere over the Pennines. We had to wait several hours for a replacement, which developed a fault, struggling back to Barnsley at a snail's pace. We arrived at Court House in the early hours of the morning, where anxious fathers, some having arrived straight from the pithead, black from their shifts at the coal face, were waiting. We walked the couple of miles to our council house, along deserted streets.'

Nearby: The contemporary 'Dragon' sculpture on the Sheffield bound platform of Barnsley Interchange becomes a row of waiting passengers when seen from a different angle.

> **The Courthouse, 24 Regent Street, Barnsley, South Yorkshire, S70 2HG. Tel. 01226 779056. Daily 9am – 11pm (Friday and Saturday midnight).**
> **www.wearinns.co.uk**

BATH (GREEN PARK), SOMERSET (station closed)

Former terminus of the Midland Railway branch from Mangotsfield.

GREEN PARK BRASSERIE AND BAR

The Somerset & Dorset Joint Railway (S&DJR) is held in high regard by enthusiasts and it is fitting that this elegant terminus (operated jointly with the Midland but the rails lifted long ago) is still busy with people. The Brasserie and Bar occupies the former booking hall, while the train-shed is used for a weekly market and as a stage for community events as well as being a supermarket car park. Gaze out from the bar to this cavernous space from which the 'Pines Express' would depart, *en route* from the North, its carriages often busy with Bournemouth-bound holidaymakers, until the 1960s. The building, with its two-storey classical façade Grade II listed, was constructed for the Midland Railway and opened as Bath Queen Square in 1869. The S&DJR arrived to share the facilities in 1874.

Though a restaurant, drinkers are also welcome, along with

Top: *Green Park Station was an imposing calling point for the* Pines Express: *now it is home to a brasserie and bar.*

Above: *The train-shed has survived but these tracks are long gone: BR 5MT No.73012 departs Bath Green Park on September 9, 1963.*

those seeking afternoon tea. Decorated in contemporary fashion, with a tiled floor and cerise coloured walls decorated with modern art for sale, there is a large photograph of the station in steam days and a British Railways wall clock, set above the wood-panelled bar counter. In a corner room is a bookcase whose contents customers may browse and some more railway-era photos. Outdoor drinkers can choose between the frontage, under the original *porte-cochère* (vehicle porch), and an area under the vast train-shed to the rear. Local Butcombe Bitter is the only real ale usually available, with Veltins imported German Pilsener on tap. I watched the sun go down, lights under the canopy brighten and, as candles on the tables flickered, I'm sure I heard the distant sound of a steam train. That beer must have been stronger than its 4 per cent ABV suggested! Cuisine is English and mainly locally sourced: diners are recommended to book. There is background music, and live jazz is staged on several evenings.

The station: The glazed, vaulted iron train-shed, its central span measuring 66 feet, is set on hexagonal columns. Beneath are vaults, once used for secure goods such as whisky, and still containing tracks. Summer Saturdays saw up to 20 express departures, until 1966 when the station was closed. Though the site came close to dereliction, its £1.5 million restoration was in 1982 and a foyer display tells the story.

Green Park Brasserie and Bar, Green Park Road, Bath, Somerset, BA1 1JB. Tel. 01225 338565. Monday 10.30am – 3pm, Tuesday to Saturday 10.30am – 10pm or later, Sunday 10.30 – 3pm. Bath Spa, on the London Paddington to Bristol Temple Meads main line, is about 12 minutes' walk. www.greenparkbrasserie.com

BEESTON, NOTTINGHAMSHIRE

Former Midland Railway main line from to London St Pancras, one stop south of Nottingham.

VICTORIA HOTEL

This former railway hotel, opened in 1899, has a patio garden so close it almost seems part of platform one of the Grade II listed Midland station. The Victoria is filled with antique signs, showcards and mirrors emblazoned with the names of vanished breweries and beers. Vallance's Best, Simpson's Double Stout and Hardy's Starbright are remembered in the advertisements; others recall Fremlin's, Waller's and Stretton's. They may have gone, but this is a haven for lovers of today's micro-brews, being a free house serving, on my visit, 14 ales including examples from Castle Rock, Hop Back, Holden's and Thornbridge, plus dark ales from Blackfriars and Burton Bridge. There are

draught German and Belgian beers plus malt whisky, farmhouse cider and wine aficionados are also well catered for. Outdoors, customers enjoy a clear view of the trains rolling by. There are two bars, both enhanced by etched windows, one of which is original, with stained-glass leaded lights. The public bar is quarry-tiled, lined with bench seating, a large Worthington Ales mirror prominent. The other, the former smoke room, has parquet flooring and an array of blackboards announcing the beers, wines and menu. This leads to further rooms which are progressively more 'diner orientated': but this is a drinker's as well as a diner's delight. Dogs welcome.

The frontage is of bright red brickwork with Jacobean style gables and period lettering, cast-iron lamp brackets and commemorative stones. There are live music nights and beer and music festivals. The pub is situated in a cul-de-sac and is best accessed (for the able-bodied) via a footbridge from the road beside the London end of platform two. Parking is limited.

The station: Dating from 1847 it features tall gables with ornate bargeboards, lozenge patterned windows, glazed awning and distinctive platform shelters. Stone shields on the gables display the initials 'MR' and the construction date.

Victoria Hotel, 85 Dovecote Lane, Beeston, Nottingham, NG9 1JG. Tel. 0115 925 4049. Monday to Saturday 10.30am – 11pm, Sunday noon – 11pm. www.victoriabeeston.co.uk

The Victoria Hotel's public bar is filled with reminders of vanished breweries.

The Centenary Lounge.

BIRMINGHAM (MOOR STREET), WEST MIDLANDS

Former Great Western Railway between Tyseley and Birmingham (Snow Hill).

CENTENARY LOUNGE (LICENSED, NO REAL ALE)

Step back to the Art Deco opulence of the 1930s in a convincing recreation of a GWR refreshment room. Polished wall panelling in walnut burr, lined with a lighter wood, lend the trade-mark 'chocolate and cream' look, complete with chrome accessories, mirrors and light fittings of the period. The familiar GWR roundel, known by staff as the 'shirt button', graces a mirrored bar back, windows and even the welcome mat. This welcoming oasis, on the concourse of one of the country's best restored main line stations (it gained a Railway Heritage Trust Conservation Award in 2004), contrasts dramatically with the modern architecture of the Selfridges store towering nearby.

The refreshment room is not a restoration but was created from scratch in the space once occupied by the 'general' and ladies' waiting rooms. The Lounge opened in June 2009 for the station's centenary, though is named in honour of the GWR's 1935 centenary. It is the brainchild of entrepreneur Aasia Baig, for which it is a labour of love. She took inspiration from the refreshment room on platform two at Leamington Spa (on the same line to the south) built in 1938 and surviving almost intact. The liberal use of mirrors was an idea gleaned from the former GWR Hotel at Paddington, another Art Deco gem. Aasia commissioned the replica features after extensive research. There are two original features. The rosewood and marble fire surround once graced a director's office at Paddington, while a vintage GWR route map was obtained at auction.

Fair trade coffee and speciality teas are served and the menu includes sandwiches, baguettes, paninis, jacket potatoes and salads – using period-style crockery based on that once used by GWR Hotels. Copies of the latter, including plates, tea-sets and teapots, produced under licence from the National Railway Museum, are sold as gift items. English and vegetarian breakfasts are available from opening time and the snack menu until closing, while cream teas provide another 'nod' to the chosen era. There is an 'outdoor' seating area on the concourse. Wine and bottled beer is served.

The station: With its handsome red brick frontage, enhanced with round-headed windows and road-side canopy, the Grade II listed terminus part of this station was built by the GWR in 1909 and closed in 1987. After a period of decline and near dereliction it was restored to its former glory, with the help of experts from Tyseley Locomotive Works, down to reproduction signage, seating and lighting. Entrance gates are from the original Snow Hill Station. It cost a cool £11 million and reopened in 2003. There is a large water tank and water crane on the terminal platforms, which also feature reproduction lamp standards and canopies. Platforms three and four were brought back into railway use in 2010. On summer Sundays, the steam-hauled Shakespeare Express calls at the adjacent through platforms. New Street Station is five minutes' walk.

Centenary Lounge, Moor Street Station, Queensway, Birmingham, B4 7UL. Tel. 0121 633 4274. Monday to Saturday 6.15am – 9pm (Fri./Sat. 9.30pm), Sunday 8.30am – 9pm. www.centenarylounge.com

BLYTHE BRIDGE (CAVERSWALL ROAD), STAFFORDSHIRE

Terminus of the Foxfield Railway, a heritage line. (Blythe Bridge main line station is a half-mile distant.)

REAL ALE TRAIN AND ONE LEGGED SHUNTER

With a name that would be quite at home on an engine from the *Thomas the Tank Engine* stories, *Florence* No.2, an 0-6-0 tank, whistles away from Caverswall Road Station to amble through the Staffordshire Moorlands. On board the two maroon carriages is a gathering of enthusiasts, a four-piece amateur folk band and a barrel of ale from the local Titanic Brewery. As the wheels roll, and a young mother reads her five year-old a story from the Reverend Awdry's repertoire in the corridor coach, the first pints are carefully dispensed in the luggage compartment of the Mark I brake second (soft drinks are also available). The band strikes up *Hello Mary Lou* and song-sheets are handed to the assembled gathering. For a brief moment I imagine we are hobos riding a freight train across a North American prairie but the dream is shattered as we pull into 'Hanbury Halt'. This was where a crinolined Dame Judi Dench and fellow actors boarded

The One Legged Shunter is housed in this station building which appears to be old but was constructed in 1995.

a vintage train in a Christmas 2009 episode of the BBC's costume drama *Cranford*. (The halt is actually Dilhorne Park, but the guard informs us the railway has kept the BBC's sign, along with a mocked-up crashed wagon nearby, as curiosities.) Ahead, down one of the steepest adhesion worked gradients in the country, an Alpine-like one-in-19, is the former Foxfield Colliery – the line's *raison d'être* until closure in 1965. It was coal rather than passengers that paid the line's bills.

After two round trips over the two-and-a-half mile route we return to Caverswall and the One Legged Shunter. This small bar is set in a corner of a new terminus building constructed in 1995. The Shunter is rudimentary but homely, as befitting an end-of-track railwayman's den. Its walls are lined with cast-iron wagon plates and signs from the LMS and North Staffordshire railway companies. There are photos of the railway and colliery in the days when coal was king and, as if to emphasise this link, a solid fuel stove provides the heat on cooler evenings. The name recalls a superstition, dating from the 1950s, that the colliery is haunted by an employee who died in an accident. His colleagues dubbed the unfortunate soul 'the one-legged shunter'.

Up to four local ales are served, often including examples from Titanic, Burton Bridge, Townhouse or Blythe Brewery or further afield (Otley O2 from Wales on my visit). Meals are available in an adjacent cafeteria until late afternoon. There is a veranda where customers can enjoy views of the workshops and servicing tracks where engines start and finish their duties. The line is known for its collection of industrial rolling stock, including the tank engine *Bellerophon*, built in 1874.

Foxfield Railway, Caverswall Road Station, Blythe Bridge, Staffordshire, ST11 9BG. Tel. 01782 396210/259667. The One Legged Shunter is open all year, Friday 6 – 11pm, weekends 11am – 11pm. The Real Ale Train runs occasionally; please contact the railway for details. www.foxfieldrailway.co.uk

BRIDGNORTH, SHROPSHIRE

Terminus of the Severn Valley Railway (formerly GWR) a heritage line from Kidderminster.

RAILWAYMAN'S ARMS

The Severn Valley Railway not only evokes the glory days of the Great Western but also boasts excellent, and contrasting, pubs at both ends of its 16-mile route. The licensed refreshment room, now called the Railwayman's Arms, on platform one of this grey sandstone, Jacobean style station, is the more historic of the two, dating from 1861. With something of a reputation for 'never closing', it completed 150 years of unbroken service in 2011. The establishment remained when the British Railways line closed to passengers and most freight in 1963. When heritage railway services began in 1970 it was a focal point for celebrations. Again, when track washouts caused a partial line closure north of Bewdley in 2007, the hospitality continued.

A cosy bolt-hole, filled with railway memorabilia and serving a delectable variety of ale, its popularity is such that, during holidays and at weekends, you will not find a seat easily. Far better to go at a quieter time and examine this veritable museum at leisure. There were seven real ales available on my last visit (including two milds) all from independent breweries. Two were from local company Bewdley, others from White Horse, Hobsons, RCH, Ironbridge and Bathams. There were also Belgian bottled beers, with draught Belgian Floreffe lager, perry and Weston's cider. To take drinks on board trains, ask for a disposable glass.

There are two drinking areas. The first room, entered from the platform, is the original bar with original cast-iron fire surround (coal fire in winter) and exemplary Smethwick's Brewery mirror above. A larger room, where the modern counter is situated, was adapted later when the pub was extended. There are 27 totem station signs decorating the rooms, with examples from all six British Railways regions of the early 1960s (the eagle-eyed will also spot a notice detailing the location of all the stations represented, enabling you to sound knowledgeable if you consult

The Railwayman's Arms.

it surreptitiously!). Other memorabilia includes railway prints and posters, loco and signal box name and number plates (the one for High Wycombe Middle Signal Box being particularly expansive) block telegraph instruments, two working antique telephones and an engraved plaque for Worthington's brewery. There are no meals served but snacks include pork pies. A CAMRA beer festival is held annually, usually in September. Children and dogs welcome; limited outdoor seating.

Nearby: England's only remaining inland funicular railway, the Bridgnorth Cliff Railway, linking High and Low Towns. Scaling 111ft-high sandstone cliffs by means of two carriages which counterbalance each other as they ascend and descend. This novel means of transport was sold to new owners in 2011.

Railwayman's Arms, Bridgnorth Station, Hollybush Road, Bridgnorth, Shropshire, WV16 5DT. Tel. 01746 764361. Monday to Thursday 11.30am – 4pm, 6-11pm, Friday 11.30am – 11pm, Saturday 11am – 11pm, Sunday noon – 10.30pm. www.svr.co.uk

BRIDLINGTON, EAST YORKSHIRE

Former York & North Midland Railway (NER)
between Hull and Scarborough.

STATION REFRESHMENT ROOMS

Part of the Grade II listed station, this is 'the UK's last example of a working railway buffet to survive intact from pre-war times' (David Gamston, editor, *Yorkshire's Real Heritage Pubs,* St. Albans 2011, page 28). Another contender is at Stalybridge (see page 110) but that has seen some changes. The station buildings date from 1912, though the two-storey section with the buffet is an extension designed in 1922 and built three years later. There are two areas, the bar which was originally for first class passengers, and the café, which was third class. Both are resplendent with original mahogany fittings, marble-topped counters and terrazzo floors. As well as these fittings (though sadly the lighting is no longer gas powered and old fireplaces have gone), the walls are festooned with railway signs, engine nameplates, wagon plates and enamel advertising signs. There is a display cabinet of model locomotives and a miniature traction engine. The café section has a collection of vintage teapots and bottles.

The refreshment rooms have been well restored over the last few years and the observant will spot details such as the British Railways insignia embellishing the food cabinet. In 2006 the bar was renovated with help from the Friends of the buffet, who also hold regular talks and film presentations on various aspects of local and transport history. Up to four real ales are available, with the focus on Yorkshire beers, though there were only two available on my visit, both from Copper Dragon of Skipton. Speciality coffees and other hot drinks and food are available at most times, ranging from sandwiches to home-roast ham, home-made pies and fresh fish. A take-away service is popular in the mornings. 'Outside'

Top left: *The first class bar at Bridlington in 2007.*
Lower left: *The café, looking towards the first class bar, in 2006.*

seating and toilets are located on the concourse.

The station: Though the imposing train-shed was demolished in the early 1960s, the surviving platforms have NER style glazed awnings on iron columns, while the main concourse is expansive and covered with a curving roof. It is a riot of colour in the summer, when the floral displays are a regular prize winner. The booking office retains decorative features in buff terracotta and wood, while the former parcels office, still with its old weighing machine, is now used by a local charity, hosting craft exhibitions and other events. The main entrance, of brick and terracotta, sports a gabled frontage, white canopy and clock.

Station Refreshment Rooms, Station Approach, Bridlington, YO15 3EP. Tel. 01262 673709. Monday to Saturday 8am – 7pm (licensed from 9am), Sunday 9.45am – 8.15pm (opening hours can vary seasonally). www.stationbuffet.com

BRISTOL (TEMPLE MEADS), BRISTOL

Former Great Western Railway main line from London Paddington and other routes.

BONAPARTES CAFÉ BAR (NO REAL ALE)

A sympathetically renovated former GWR refreshment room, in part of Sir Matthew Digby Wyatt's 1878 through station enlargement of Brunel's original terminus. The latter includes the Gothic station entrance still in use. The spacious room is of brick, with curving Gothic window frames of stone on two levels and a high ceiling supported on heavy beams. It resembles a medieval hall, albeit one that has had a twentieth century makeover.

The tiled floor has a chequerboard central feature and the contemporary wooden bar counter with its mirrored back is in keeping with the historical setting. Half the room is set with

Bonapartes has the look of a medieval great hall.

sofas and low tables and chairs, while the other is furnished with dining tables and chairs. Here, one can gaze through the windows to the 500ft. long curving train-shed, also of 1878, and four of the station's through tracks. There is an 'outside' dining area on the platform, under the train-shed roof. Beside the bar entrance is the framed GWR Roll of Honour, listing 2,436 company staff lost in the Great War of 1914-18 while, inside, are two period-style wall clocks. A tall stand with magazines and newspapers for sale, and two games machines, are the most jarring objects to spoil an otherwise sympathetic renovation. The bar is licensed but the range of drinks is not as wide as most pubs. A snack menu is served until the evening (Sunday 4pm). I found the place clean and bright, with friendly staff. There are 'phone and computer recharge points and toilets.

The station: The oldest part of Temple Meads is I.K. Brunel's original terminus, built in 1840, adjacent to the current station and Grade I listed. One of the world's oldest railway termini, railway use ended in 1965. Behind the Tudor-style frontage and former railway offices in Temple Gate is a remarkable mock-Tudor train-shed, complete with Brunel's *faux* hammer-beam roof which spanned five broad gauge tracks. Though partly used as a car park, it has recently been employed for beer festivals by the local branch of CAMRA.

Bonapartes Café Bar, Platform 3, Bristol Temple Meads Station, Bristol, BS1 6QG. Tel. 0117 925 5308 or 2953.
Monday to Saturday 7am – 9.30pm,
Sunday 8am – 9pm.

BROCKFORD, SUFFOLK

Former Mid-Suffolk Light Railway between Haughley and Laxfield (closed).
Part reopened as a heritage line.

THE MIDDY BAR

A unique hostelry housed in a wood-bodied passenger coach built in 1876, adjacent to a working reconstruction of an Edwardian light railway station. It is one of those places where a comment about anything to do with trains or beer will trigger a friendly conversation and, stepping aboard, I was transported (not literally, for it is a grounded coach body) back to an age when lines of this kind were run on a shoestring and a bare-boards pub was at the heart of every rural community.

The bar is run by volunteers and its home, a Great Eastern four-wheel, five compartment third class coach (No. 278T), was one of a pair discovered in use as bungalow extensions in Acle. Its companion, No.287, is fully restored as a MSLR vehicle and can be ridden on the museum's quarter-mile line. The 'bar' retains its original frame but, though barely rain-tight, will one day be restored to running order, at which stage it will be

The Middy Bar is an ancient third class coach carefully converted for real ale lovers.

replaced by a GE six-wheel coach of 1892, No.424, observed as a shell waiting patiently under a tarpaulin for its day in the limelight. So, I was assured, there will always be a Middy Bar though, like a hermit crab, its home may change. The furnishings are simple wooden kitchen chairs and tables, set with gingham table-cloths, with a home-made wooden bar at one end and a set of black-and-white photos of the original line at the other. Shove ha'penny can be played.

Ales are served by gravity direct from the cask, with three East Anglian examples usually available, notably from Suffolk breweries Earl Soham (Woodbridge) and/or Cliff Quay (Ipswich). On my visit Crouch Vale's Brewer's Gold was also served. The compact stillage, cooled in warm weather by a portable air-conditioning system and damp towels, has capacity for eight casks, and this number of beers is available during an annual beer festival in late August. An unusual feature is that one beer is kept in a specially adapted metal pin (a four-and-a-half gallon cask) engraved 'MSLR', which is refilled by the brewery and is more economical than the larger firkin.

The only concessions to the twenty-first century are electric lighting (basic) and a coffee machine (small). There is an outdoor seating area next to another GE coach, built in 1863 and second oldest in the country (this is due to be shunted along to make more space). It is a sign of the times that the village, which once had four pubs, now has none, so the bar opens on a few summer evenings for the locals, as well as for private functions. On one occasion a 'twilight evening' was held, with station oil lamps lit. No meals are served but there's a barbeque on opening days, and the museum has a refreshment room. There's no ambient music, just the sound of the steam train. Children are welcome. Drinks can be taken on the train and take-away beer is available. Toilets are in the nearby museum.

The station: The Mid-Suffolk Light Railway Museum is recreating the atmosphere of a little-known rural line that ran 'from nowhere to the middle of a field' (it left the London to Norwich main line at Haughley, north of Stowmarket) from 1904 to 1952. Optimistic directors had intended to continue eastwards and link with the iconic Southwold Railway which, after its conversion to standard gauge, would have provided access to a port. The station uses original corrugated iron and matchwood buildings and is served by a tank engine and four-wheel coaches in distinctive reddy-brown livery. Though the ride is short, it is a commendable recreation of an Edwardian make-do-and-mend railway long gone from rural England.

> **The Middy Bar, Mid-Suffolk Light Railway Museum, Wetheringsett, Stowmarket, Suffolk, IP14 5PW. Tel. 01449 766899. Open on certain Sundays and Bank Holiday Mondays, from May to November, 11am – 5pm. Museum admission charge payable. Nearest station: Stowmarket, then taxi. www.mslr.org.uk**

No, it's not 1904: this is Brockford in 2010, and the Middy Bar is behind the corrugated iron station building.

BUILTH ROAD, POWYS

Former Cambrian Railways between Moat Lane Junction and Three Cocks (closed). Adjacent high level station (open) on former London & North Western Railway, the Heart of Wales line, between Craven Arms and Swansea.

CAMBRIAN ARMS (NO REAL ALE)

This former railway refreshment room, which once formed the nucleus of the lower of two stations, continues as a friendly pub though the railway it served closed almost 50 years ago. Located in one of the most remote and scenic parts of Wales, the twin Builth Road stations were a busy meeting place for two competing railways. Only one survives, that serving the former LNWR single line established to compete with the GWR for South Wales coal traffic and now providing a rural ride *par excellence:* the Heart of Wales line. Passengers on the diesel units making their 120-mile cross-country amble may barely glimpse a long, whitewashed and slate roofed building below them at this point. This is the former low level station, initially named

'Llechryd for Central Wales', on the erstwhile Mid Wales Railway opened in 1861. It weaved its way south from Moat Lane to Three Cocks, another remote junction. It was operated by the Cambrian Railways from 1888, the station being renamed Builth Road, like its neighbour, soon after. The refreshment room was just the place to linger if you were changing trains. Railway enthusiasts found it an idyllic place to quench their thirst on balmy summer afternoons. The station and its connecting routes shut for good in 1962.

There are two rooms, one akin to a domestic lounge, complete with sofa and dartboard, and the other the main bar, with its original counter and furnished with benches and tables. Historical local photographs show the stations in their heyday, when a luggage lift linked the platforms, there were rows of cattle pens, goods yards and engine sheds where banking engines waited to help heavy freights up the gradients. There are also collections of hurricane lamps, blowlamps earthenware pots and, in the lounge, a faded GWR illustrated map of the Cambrian Coast, promoting holiday travel by rail. Two real fires keep the place warm in winter. Landlady Angie Mason serves lunchtime meals including a popular Sunday roast for which booking is advised. No background music; this is a place for

The Cambrian Arms with a train for Shrewsbury entering the high level station in February 2011. The Cambrian Railways lines once ran in the foreground.

Right: *The bar of the Cambrian Arms, the former station refreshment room.*

British Railways 2MT class No.46510 enters Builth Road (low level) shortly before closure in 1962. The refreshment room is just out of shot to the left.

conversation. There is outside seating and a railway style smokers' shelter. Part of the building housed a shop which closed a decade ago. Rail travellers should note: Builth is a request stop and there are only four trains each way daily.

Nearby: Though partly obscured by road improvements, it is possible to walk part of the former Cambrian Railways route, following the River Wye, into Builth Wells, a former spa town. This can be joined beside the A470, half-a-mile north of the Royal Welsh Showground.

Cambrian Arms, Builth Road, Builth Wells, Powys, LD2 3RG (off A470 north of Builth Wells). Tel. 01982 553200. Monday to Friday noon – 2pm, 6 – 10.30pm, Saturday noon – 2.30pm, 7 – 11pm, Sunday noon – 2.30pm.

BURY (BOLTON STREET), GREATER MANCHESTER

Former East Lancashire Railway (later Lancashire & Yorkshire) now terminus of the East Lancashire Railway, a heritage line to Rawtenstall.

THE TRACKSIDE

Situated on one of England's premier preserved railways, this free house serves an array of ales as steam locomotives simmer outside. Though only licensed in 2004 and set in a modern brick building, part of it has an older ancestry. The platform-side façade originally graced offices at the Bury Corporation Tramways Depot but was dismantled brick-by-brick and re-erected at this site in the early 1990s. The composite building, which also houses a kitchen, toilets and mess-room, stands on the site of the original ELR headquarters of 1847, an edifice in the Palladian style that included a booking office, company offices and board room, and the obligatory refreshment room. It was demolished in the 1970s – a new concourse at street level having replaced it in 1952.

Nine beer pumps were serving ales from breweries including Skipton, Tring, Robinsons and B&T on my visit. There are also

The Trackside in 2005.

continental bottled beers. Plastic glasses are issued for those drinking outside on the platform, where there are seats and tables giving a ringside view of the trains. The menu is traditional pub fare such as cottage pie and fish and chips; the breakfasts are hearty and there are hot filled muffins and jacket potatoes. Food is served Wednesday to Friday lunchtimes and at weekends until 4pm.

The single large room has a tiled floor and walls decorated with railway prints, beer mats and pump clips, many affixed high in the pitched ceiling. A radio provided background music. Toilets are on the platform. Children are welcome until early evening. An easy walk from the Metrolink tram from central Manchester.

Nearby: The ELR provides a scenic excursion behind vintage steam and diesel engines, running 12 miles along the Irwell Valley to Heywood and Rawtenstall. At Heywood, the Pheonix Brewery of 1898, closed by Bass in the 1960s, has been restored and is brewing once again, while a Rawtenstall attraction is Fitzpatrick's, Britain's last remaining temperance bar.

> **The Trackside Bar, Platform Two, East Lancashire Railway, Bury, Lancashire BL9 0EY. Tel. 0161 764 6461. Monday to Friday, noon – midnight, Saturday, 9am – 12.30am, Sunday 9am – 11.30pm. www.eastlancsrailway.org.uk**

CARNFORTH, LANCASHIRE

Former London & North Western, Furness and Midland Railway Joint, between Lancaster/Morecambe and Barrow-in-Furness/Leeds

BRIEF ENCOUNTER REFRESHMENT ROOM (LICENSED, NO REAL ALE)

As I sipped my Jennings Cumberland ale and wondered what it was like when David Lean's 1945 film *Brief Encounter* was shot here, I heard the unmistakable sound of a steam locomotive. I was not dreaming: West Coast Railways maintain the locomotives they use for main-line excursions behind the station, in the engine servicing depot once known as Steamtown, long since closed to the public. Lean used express trains billowing steam and smoke, assisted by Rachmaninov's powerful accompaniment, to help symbolise Laura and Alec's growing feelings for each other in this tale of a love that was not to be. Based on the stage play *Still Life* by Noel Coward, this is the station on which much of it was filmed towards the end of World War II – representing the fictional Milford Junction. The refreshment room where key scenes are played out has been carefully re-created. The expresses still thunder past as they did in the film, except they are now electric Pendolinos rather than Stanier Pacifics and the mainline platforms were removed in 1970, prior to electrification of this stretch of the West Coast main line. But the station clock, built by Joyce of Whitchurch, fully restored and wound by hand weekly, still hangs above the sloping subway ramp where the film's passengers rushed to and fro, while piles of vintage suitcases await a non-existent porter.

With its wooden floor and polished bar counter complete with period cash register showing pounds, shillings and pence, and stainless steel hot water urns, it is a plausible representation of the buffet used in the film. Movie historians will tell you that the interiors were shot at Denham Studios in Buckinghamshire and the exterior views, though filmed at Carnforth, used prefabricated film 'flats' on the station: but both were based on the genuine article at Carnforth. The station was chosen in preference to one near London as it was, by that stage in the war, safe from enemy attack. All filming took place at night so it would not interfere with railway operations. The place is not exactly like that where Laura (Celia Johnson) and Alec (Trevor Howard) met. The absence of hand-pumps on the counter (even dummy ones) is one example. This is a real 'one off', however, a remarkable place which has been restored from a state of almost total dereliction and enhanced by its visitor centre, run by enthusiastic volunteers. There are annual 1940s events, when

At Brief Encounter it seems time has stood still in 1945.

built the main Tudor-style buildings, on what is now an island platform where the Refreshment Room is situated, for the Lancaster & Carlisle Railway. The Furness Railway arrived in 1857, followed by the Furness & Midland in 1867, and the LNWR and LMSR also successively put their stamp on the place. The main entrance building beside the southbound main line was not added until the early 1880s. Among the payload were thousands of troops who used the station in both World Wars. In 1942 a second Furness platform was added by the LMS to cope with wartime traffic. The 1960s saw a steady decline in importance and physical deterioration. After many years lying derelict, a ten year old dream to restore the station reached an important stage in 2000 when a £1.5 million refurbishment was unveiled, with the visitor facilities opening three years later. (The VIP guest at the reopening ceremony was Margaret Barton, last surviving character from Lean's film.) Naturally, the Visitor Centre, housed in the restored station, includes a *Brief Encounter* exhibition, with photographs, descriptions and mementoes of the film and its local connections. A letter home written by Celia Johnson during the making of the film affirms 'I have got awfully fond of Carnforth Station...'

Other rooms recount the town's importance in two World Wars and the history of both town and railway. At the far end of the building is the Furness and Midland Hall, where the booking office was once situated and functions and film shows are now staged. With its high, beamed roof it is quite church-like. At the northern (Barrow) end of the station is a tall, Tudor-style building with decorative chimney. This is the original Furness Railway signal box, built in the 1870s. For the benefit of real ale fans, The Snug Micropub opened on the station in summer 2012. Admission to the site and exhibition is free.

enthusiasts come dressed in period costume, and monthly jazz nights.

Tea is served in white china pots and freshly ground coffee and wine is available. A menu of light meals is complemented by an assortment of home-made cakes and pastries including scones and cream, with bread, cakes and scones baked on the premises. The 'stationmaster's office' is furnished with armchairs and a solid fuel stove. There is 'outdoor' seating under the station awning on the platform, separated from the trains by white picket fencing.

The station: Carnforth grew into a major junction over many years, becoming an east-west and north-south railway crossroads, though it retrenched when the West Coast main line platforms were closed, necessitating a detour south to Lancaster for those wishing to head north towards Carlisle. There has been a station here since 1846, when Sir William Tite

> **Brief Encounter Refreshment Room, Platform One, Carnforth Station, Warton Road, Carnforth, Lancashire, LA5 9TR. Tel. 01524 732432. Daily, 8am (9am Sunday) – 4pm. www.refreshmentroom.com**

CHAPPEL & WAKES COLNE, ESSEX

Former Colchester, Stour Valley, Sudbury & Halstead Railway (GER) between Marks Tey and Sudbury. Home of the East Anglian Railway Museum.

THE SHUNTERS ARMS

One has to time a visit to this compact drinking den carefully, as it only opens for five days a year, during the summer beer festival. Proving that the best pubs don't have to be fancy affairs, it consists of a vintage Southern Railway parcels van, entered from the platform via a ramp. A home-made servery, complete with two hand-pumps, is set at one end of the wagon, with a range of other ales served direct from barrels racked behind it. There are a couple of plastic chairs for customers, but most prefer to stand (three is a crowd) on the wooden floor, or use the ample seating provided in an open wagon and passenger coach stabled nearby.

Despite its diminutive size, the Shunters serves up to 12 micro-brewery ales, often including examples from Crouch Vale, Nethergate and Mauldons. Due to a fast turnover, the beers are always in tip-top condition. No food is served. Toilets are a short walk away: male customers can avail themselves of an ornate open-air pissoir, which once graced Cockfield Station in Suffolk, on the platform.

The Shunters was initially based in a four-wheel BR standard 12-ton box van built in 1952 for general goods work. The bar's requirements and popularity outgrew this so, in 2010, it was transferred to the current, larger home: a pre-war, ex-SR PMV (Parcels and Miscellaneous Van) as once used on boat trains to Southampton and Dover. Beer is kept cool using a water chiller feeding water to cooling jackets on the casks. This quirky bar is one of the highlights of beer festivals that have been run by the Essex branches of CAMRA at the East Anglian Railway Museum for 25 years. Further bars, serving 400 ales from local breweries and rare beers not normally available in the county, are situated in the Restoration Shed (where rail equipment is in various stages of rebuilding) and in and outside the Goods Shed. Decorated with enamel BR Eastern Region signs and a wooden crane, this was once served by a daily goods train.

It is a rare pleasure to be able to drink (and eat a variety of hot food) *al fresco,* immersed in this evocative railway setting, surrounded by rolling stock, signs and other artefacts. It is also a novelty to step off the single-unit diesel train from Marks Tey (connection from Liverpool Street and Colchester) straight into this almost theatrical scene, crossing the tracks via a covered footbridge originally at Stowmarket. Chappel's red brick station building, with an ornate platform canopy, dates from the early 1890s, though the booking hall is restored to 1950s vintage. An unusual feature: its main entrance is on the upper-storey rather than at ground level.

Nearby: The 32-arch Chappel Viaduct, built of local brick in 1849, carries the railway 75 feet above the Colne Valley.

Imbibing at the Shunters is a rare experience: note the open wagon for outdoor drinkers.

East Anglian Railway Museum, Chappel & Wakes Colne Station, Essex CO6 2DS. Tel. 01206 242524. The Shunters Arms opens as part of a five-day beer festival in early September. Admission charge. www.earm.co.uk

CLEETHORPES (LAKESIDE), LINCOLNSHIRE (1)

On the Cleethorpes Coast Light Railway,
a privately run miniature line.

THE SIGNAL BOX INN

This diminutive hostelry, opened in 2006, calls itself 'the smallest pub on the planet.' The claim is contentious though there's no doubt more than four customers seated and two standing does make it rather crowded. Once you've settled down with a beer, however, such as one from the Tom Woods range brewed in Grimsby, or one of eight ciders, you will agree that 'the best things come in small packages'. In this case, eight feet by eight feet. The building has genuine railway ancestry, having been the signal cabin at Stanton sidings, Scunthorpe. The original stove was removed and a counter, beer-pulls and satellite television receiver added. Instead of a cellar, beer casks are stored in a low, brick-built extension, accessed via a lifting flap. Real ale festivals are held.

The Lilliputian theme continues outside, the hostelry being situated beside the main station of the Cleethorpes Coast Light Railway, a two-mile miniature line of 15-inch gauge. It is the last surviving seaside steam railway on the east coast. The station incorporates many features found at standard gauge stations, including a train-shed, a tea-room and a stack of baggage awaiting shipment. The country's first museum devoted to miniature railways is being established here. The only things not reduced in scale are the passengers and the pints: it is reminiscent of a scene from *Alice's Adventures in Wonderland.* Meals are served in the adjacent Teapot Café.

The railway dates from 1948 when it was built by the council but it is now privately run with the help of a Supporters' Association. An interesting rolling stock collection includes that of the long closed Sutton Miniature Railway from Sutton Coldfield which had been in storage for 40 years but is being restored. To reach the inn, join one of the CCLR trains from Kingsway terminus, situated under a mile south-east of

The Signal Box Inn.

the main-line station (see next page). Buses 8, 9 (17 in summer) also pass the railway.

Nearby: A distinctive, iron-framed glass and wood structure on the North Promenade, now the Mermaid Restaurant, was once a railway refreshment room. Built by Lockerbie and Wilkinson, who were also responsible for the main-line station's clock tower but were better known for penny-in-the-slot machines. It was sold by the London & North Eastern Railway in 1936.

The Signal Box Inn, Lakeside Station, King's Road, Cleethorpes, Lincolnshire DN35 0AG. Tel. 01472 604657. Daily except Mondays, Easter to October (weekends only early and late season) 11am – 11pm. www.cleethorpescoastlightrailway.co.uk

CLEETHORPES, LINCOLNSHIRE (2)

Terminus of former Manchester Sheffield and
Lincolnshire Railway (GCR) from Grimsby.

NUMBER ONE & NUMBER TWO REFRESHMENT ROOMS

With two independent and contrasting pubs, in different parts of
a station comprised of a collection of buildings from several
periods, this is a rare location indeed. The Number One is situated
in the early station buildings dating from 1863 (it opened with
this single platform) though the interior has been modernized.
Spacious and split into three drinking areas, three real ales,
Everard's Tiger, Tom Woods and Ruddles County were available
on my visit. There is a children's room and outside seating
(roadside). Ambient music; no meals except Sunday lunch.

The Number Two is situated on the concourse in the shadow
of the station's landmark clock tower of 1884. A one-roomed
hostelry, constructed as part of a 1960s' modernization, it is
small but well laid-out with upholstered benches around
the walls. A multiple CAMRA award winning pub, there are
five hand-pumps with a changing range of ales, usually
including a mild. The selection on my visit included Box
Tunnel, Hancock's HB, Hardy & Hanson's Olde Trip and
Bateman's Valiant. Ambient music; no meals served; outdoor
seating on concourse.

> **Number One Refreshment Room, Station Approach
> (Platform One), Cleethorpes, Lincolnshire, DN35 8AX.
> Daily noon – midnight (Monday 7pm). Number Two
> Refreshment Room, Station Approach, Cleethorpes,
> Lincolnshire, DN35 8AX.
> Tel. 07905 375587. Daily 7.30am – midnight.**

CODSALL, STAFFORDSHIRE

Former Shrewsbury and Birmingham Railway
(GWR) between Wolverhampton and Telford.

CODSALL STATION

With its cast-iron footbridge, white picket fencing and station
building decorated with round-headed windows and jumble of
tall chimneys, Codsall would be at home on a model railway. The
Grade II listed building, dating from 1849, was converted into a
railway themed pub by Black Country brewer Holdens in 1999.
The footbridge was rebuilt following damage by a road-rail crane
six years later (thankfully the two events are unconnected).

The combination of a popular community pub and a
working station is pleasing. A compact bar counter is set with
five hand-pumps dispensing the Holden's range (including
Mild, Bitter and Golden Glow) plus at least one guest: on my
visit this was from Burton Bridge. A row of CAMRA award
certificates is lined up above the bar, indicating the pub has
passed muster by real ale fans. All three main public areas –
comfortable lounge, compact bar with snug and quarry-tiled

*The Number One, seen in 2006, is housed in a station building altered
and extended many times since opening in 1863.*

conservatory (a modern addition) – are adorned with prints, posters and railway memorabilia, mostly of the Great Western Railway and its successors but some from overseas. They range from signal arms to enamel station totems, locomotive nameplates and numbers to cast-iron signs. The nameplates feature West Country class *Bideford,* an LNWR loco of 1875, *Snowdon* and the GWR's *Bingley Hall.* The lounge carpet features the familiar GWR motif, while posters encourage customers to enjoy the 'glorious sands of St Ives' or ride the 'new diesel expresses of 1957' while imitation gas lamps provide illumination. Outside is a raised terrace, with more station signs, giving a grandstand view of the main line. Meals

are served lunchtimes (booking recommended on Sundays) and evenings, Sundays excepted. Faggots, chips and peas are a house speciality; cod, chips and pies are popular too. There is an annual beer festival and, a rare provision at a station, a boules pitch. Ambient music.

Codsall Station, Platform Two, Chapel Lane, Codsall, Staffordshire, WV8 2EH. Tel. 01902 847061.
Monday to Thursday, 11.30am – 3, 2.30 – 11pm.
Friday and Saturday, 11.30am – 11.30pm. Sunday, noon – 10.30pm.

There's no indication from this view that Codsall Station is now a pub, nor that delights for rail and ale enthusiasts lie within. Diesel unit 170 513 enters with a train for Shrewsbury on 14 April, 2010.

CONSALL, STAFFORDSHIRE

Former North Staffordshire Railway, now the Churnet Valley Railway, a heritage line near Leek.

THE BLACK LION

Set in a hamlet in the wooded Churnet Valley, where the river, railway and the Caldon Canal are entwined, the Black Lion is a secluded retreat. The nearest surfaced road is at least half-a-mile away – neither station (to the south, five minutes' walk) nor pub allow vehicular access, the car park being the other side of the railway, canal and river. This is a rustic hostelry, built to serve local lime kiln workers and consisting of an L-shaped, quarry tiled bar with stone fireplace, leading to two further rooms, one set aside for diners.

Five hand-pumps supply unusual ales from independent breweries (though the house beer is from Tetley). On my visit these were Peakstones Rock, Alton's Black Hole, Toft Stumped, Rudgate Ruby Mild and Wyre Piddle Piddlesner. The indecisive can request a selection of three one-third pints. There were also at least two farm ciders.

Due to the railway's proximity, and the absence of a road, beer consignments often came to the Black Lion by train. This shows a delivery being made to the pub in June 1958. A similar special delivery was repeated by the CVR for a beer festival in 2009.

It was a joy to sit in the spacious garden (shared with the free-range chickens) a superb vantage point for steam train watchers. The station, with its wooden buildings and semaphore signals, is a remarkable revival, the original being demolished after its closure in the sixties. There is the sound of water tumbling over a weir and, occasionally, a narrow-boat plying the canal. Food is served daily, with Sunday hog-roasts a speciality and regular 'pie and pud' nights, quiz nights and acoustic guitar evenings. Occasional beer and cider festivals. Camping.

Nearby: Popular with walkers, local sights include the Devil's Staircase, lime kilns and a nature reserve. The CVR, running through 'Staffordshire's hidden valley,' opened as the North Staffordshire Railway in 1849. Volunteers have recreated the ambience of the 1950s/60s era. In late 2010 it was linked with the revived Cauldon Low line at Leekbrook Junction near Cheddleton. Cheddleton Flint Mill, an eighteenth century water-powered flint crushing mill, opens periodically.

The Black Lion in its woodland setting near Consall Station. The garden provides a perfect vantage point for steam train watching.

The Black Lion, Consall Forge, Wetley Rocks, Staffordshire, ST9 0AJ. (Off A522.) Tel. 01782 550294. Daily, noon – 11pm (Sunday 10.30pm). www.blacklionpub.co.uk

CREDITON, DEVON

Former Exeter & Crediton Railway (LSWR) served by Exeter to Barnstaple and Okehampton services.

STATION TEA ROOMS (UNLICENSED)

This Grade II listed station building, a Brunelian Tudor design of 1854, is now a tea-room containing a treasure-trove of railway artefacts, photographs and other ephemera. There is an 0 gauge model of the station in LSWR days in the former waiting room. Once neglected, the building was transformed into this cosy place of refreshment by Linda Rogers (now Brown) in 1996. The old booking hall is now the dining area where hot and cold snacks, including sandwiches, cheese on toast, omelettes and all-day breakfasts, including a popular Station Master's breakfast, are served along with a selection of cakes, scones, sweets and puddings. Outdoor seating in summer. See also: Newton St Cyres.

The station: A level crossing is adjacent, with a part weather-boarded signal box built in 1875. The line diverges

The Station Tea Rooms are housed in this handsome building designed in 1854.

here, one route going to Barnstaple, the other to Okehampton and Meldon Quarry. A quirk of history is that the track gauge was converted three times: from broad to standard, then back to broad and finally standard, thanks to wrangling between the GWR and LSWR.

Station Tea Rooms, Railway Station, Crediton, Devon, EX17 3BY. Tel. 01363 777766. Monday to Saturday 9am – 4pm. Sunday closed.

CRIANLARICH, PERTHSHIRE

Former North British Railway between Craigendoran and Fort William and junction for Oban.

STATION TEA ROOM (UNLICENSED)

The single-track West Highland Railway is one of the great scenic train journeys, providing a theatrical escape from bustling Glasgow (Queen Street) into wild mountains, moors and, ultimately, the Atlantic coast at Mallaig. This privately run Tea Room achieved a similarly elevated reputation, for the quality of its meal baskets, soon after the line's opening and is still popular with rail travellers and hikers. It is situated on an island platform in a whitewashed building with adjacent, platform mounted signal box. Though its furnishings and décor are modest, it is smartly kept by Gordon Gaughan who has maintained the establishment's traditions of hospitality. By necessity, the room is long and thin but its sales counter – with the all-important kitchen out of sight behind — sells a wealth of merchandise far beyond that required for mere sustenance. There are booklets, mugs, maps, videos of trains in the Highlands and steamboats on the Clyde, key-fobs and postcards – a range of souvenirs for the time-strapped tourist.

Dining cars didn't arrive on the West Highland until 1929, so from the earliest days the tea room provided meals for train-loads of hungry passengers, to be hastily consumed during a

Crianlarich Station, in its scenic Highland setting, where the Tea Room has refreshed train passengers for more than a hundred years.

The tradition of book-ahead hot meals is maintained, today's customers making contact by 'phone, facsimile or letter rather than telegram. The menu ranges from all-day breakfasts and other hot meals such as steak and kidney pie to bacon, sausage or egg rolls and even venison burgers. A summer left luggage facility is available. There is level access from the platform but that to the station is through a subway, up a flight of steps.

The station: This once boasted a turntable and multiple water columns at each end (so double-headed trains could be refreshed simultaneously) and interchange with the Caledonian Railway's Oban line which had a separate, low-level station until 1965. Crianlarich is still served by the so-called *Deerstalker Express*, a name given by the media to the overnight sleeper from London Euston on its 520-mile run to Fort William. The West Highland Way, a long distance trail using part of an old military road, reaches its halfway point nearby.

> Station Tea Room, Crianlarich Station, Perthshire, Scotland, FK20 8QN. Tel. 01838 300204. Daily except Sunday (March to end October) 7.30am – 4pm.

stop of less than 11 minutes or boxed and taken on board. Some of these were the finest of picnics, as miles of lineside either side of the station were reportedly strewn with champagne corks and the shells of plovers' eggs!

There is a display of telegrams, some more than a century old, received from passengers detailing their meal requirements. An enlightening description of this service comes from John Thomas in his history, *The West Highland Railway*:

> 'Some of the travellers took their baskets to the seclusion of their compartments, but others preferred to explore its mysteries in the open air. Many a passenger who had entrained the previous night in London enjoyed his first Scottish breakfast sitting on a platform seat at Crianlarich, his appetite whetted by the pure, crisp air of a Perthshire morning... The arrival of the trains was greeted with enthusiasm by the Crianlarich hens. The sound of an approaching train was the signal for every fowl in the railway cottage gardens to go squawking and clucking over the rails, oblivious of the danger of churning wheels, to solicit crumbs from the open-air diners.'

CROMER, NORFOLK

Former Eastern and Midlands Railway (Midland and Great Northern Joint), now served by Norwich to Sheringham 'Bittern Line' services.

NO. 98 COCKTAIL LOUNGE & BAR (No real ale)

With its sandy beaches, pier and colourful crab boats, Cromer is the so-called 'Gem of the Norfolk Coast,' though this bar in the former station is something of a curate's egg. No. 98 occupies what was the spacious Cromer Beach station building, a bold architectural statement echoing the Arts and Crafts Movement. On opening in 1887 it announced to the town's Victorian inhabitants that the railway had well and truly arrived (though the Great Eastern reached Cromer High – closed in 1954 – ten years earlier). Railway use of the building ceased (and the handsome train-shed closed off) in 1970 when it was occupied by builders' merchants Travis & Arnold. In 1998 it became a pub, the first in a number of licensed incarnations, the latest opening in 2011, a contemporary bar catering mainly for the younger set. There's an array of chrome and leather and, upstairs, a night club. No reminders at all of the days when passengers would request a return ticket to Caister-on-Sea or Melton Constable or warm themselves by the waiting room fire, maybe enjoying a pint of cask Bass Burton ale in the refreshment room that survived until 1966. Weather permitting, I recommend an *al fresco* drink, in order to savour the railway architecture, before progressing to the Suffield Arms at Gunton Station or to Sheringham for a steam interlude on the North Norfolk Railway (see next page).

The building sports diagonal courses of red brick and large half-timbered

The Arts and Crafts style Cromer Station building is cavernous.

Below: *Cromer Beach station circa 1902, with M&GN C class 4-4-0 locomotive No.5 waiting in the bay platform. Today only the bay, two tracks and the station building, minus its train shed, remain.*

gables decorated with mock timbering and brick nogging beneath. This could almost be a large villa for a well-heeled family, were it not for the handsome glass canopy over the entrance, a feature added later on its acquisition by the M&GNJR, affectionately known as the 'Muddle and Get Nowhere' due to its lightly used east-west routes, many of which closed in 1959. It is supported by cast-iron spandrels with brackets incorporating M&GN monograms. A high rear wall is the clue that the main platform was once sheltered by a train-shed, complete with EMR monogrammed brackets. Where this stood is now a car park for a supermarket which also covers the site of the goods yard, turntable and engine shed. A wooden signal box survives and dates from 1920. Alongside are preserved semaphore signals. The bar has a wide menu served until early evening. Ambient music.

Nearby: This is a stub-end station, trains having to reverse before continuing their journeys. The approach to Cromer from the south is akin to riding a switchback, the track first ascending, then descending some 200 feet as it loops through a semi-circle to join the old M&GN coastal route west of the station, coming to a halt within sight of the 160 foot-high parish church tower, the loftiest in Norfolk.

An eight minute train ride takes you to Sheringham, where the whole town turned out to see the level crossing reinstated in 2010, reuniting what is now known as the Poppy Line with the national network. This heritage railway runs through five miles of countryside from a station restored to its 1950s atmosphere (and hosting one of the bigger rail ale festivals each summer) to a gas-lit platform at Holt. This has a museum devoted to William Marriott, revered in railway circles as leading light, and Locomotive Superintendent, of the long mourned M&GNJR.

No. 98 Cocktail Lounge & Bar, The Old Station House, Holt Road, Cromer, Norfolk, NR27 9EB. Tel. 01263 514000. Daily, noon – 11pm, Friday and Saturday until 2am.

DERBY, DERBYSHIRE

Former Midland Railway main line from London (St Pancras) to Sheffield and other routes.

THE BRUNSWICK INN

Notable both for its unique railway heritage and, for the last 20 years, as a brew-pub, the fount of real ales such as Midnight Express and Railway Porter (see page 127). The Grade II listed building dates from 1842 and is believed to be the world's first purpose-built railwayman's inn. Closed in the 1970s, it reopened as a pub in the late eighties. Situated in the Railway Conservation Area, it forms part of a triangle of shops and some 80 houses originally built for railway workers by the North Midland Railway in 1841 (around the same time as the Midland Hotel which is still in business opposite the station). It is claimed to narrowly pre-date the railway village in Swindon, much to the annoyance of GWR fans.

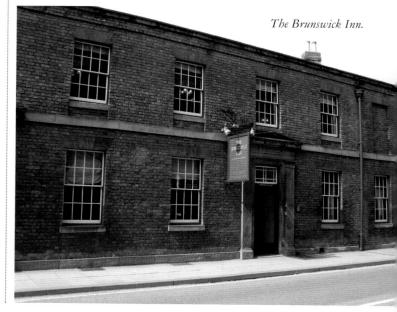

The Brunswick Inn.

The inn, part of the Everards estate since 2002, is a labyrinth of flag-stoned rooms, though there is just one bar, occupying a corner of one of the larger rooms. Real fires and sturdy wooden furniture help create a rustic cottage feel. Photos of the glory days of the Midland Railway are much in evidence along with displays about the history of the Railway Village and its restoration – at one stage this became run-down and at risk of demolition. A glazed partition provides views of the compact brewery and, on weekdays, the brewer at work. On my visit six of the superb home-brews were available, including Railway Porter and Old Accidental, as well as nine guest ales. Among them were examples from York, Fox, RCH, and Everards.

A lively community pub and CAMRA award winner, The Brunswick is well used by locals – there were two separate meetings in progress during my visit, in upstairs rooms. Jazz sessions are held; annual beer festival (September). Lunchtime meals are served daily, until late afternoon on Friday and Saturday. The varied menu includes an all-day breakfast, Cumberland Whirl with mash and onion gravy, Brunswick Pie as well as soup and jacket potatoes. Outdoor seating.

The station: Derby Midland's grand buildings suffered from World War II bomb damage, the remainder being demolished in the 1950s. The current ones date from 1985. Derby was headquarters of the Midland Railway and city and company were almost synonymous. There are plenty of reminders, though today the space taken up by railway and associated businesses is much reduced and the site of Derby Works has become a retail and commercial development. The historic locomotive Roundhouse has been converted as part of Derby College's campus.

> **The Brunswick Inn and Brewery, 1 Railway Terrace, Derby, Derbyshire, DE1 2RU. Tel. 01332 290677. (Turn right out of station forecourt and the pub is three minutes' walk.) Monday to Saturday, 11am – 11pm. Sunday, noon – 10.30pm. www.everards.co.uk**

The West Riding Licensed Refreshment Rooms.

DEWSBURY, WEST YORKSHIRE

Former London & North Western Railway between Huddersfield and Leeds.

THE WEST RIDING LICENSED REFRESHMENT ROOMS

Ensconced in part of a Tudor style, stone-built station dating from 1848, the West Riding is a thriving destination pub with a large selection of ales. At weekends it is not unusual to see each train disgorge several passengers straight into the pub as others do the opposite, heading for the next venue on the Trans-Pennine Ale Trail. Opened in 1994 when real ale enthusiast Mike Field converted the old waiting rooms, the pub became an instant success and a CAMRA award winner. Spanning three rooms, the place has retained its period character thanks to its dark wood panelling, neo-Tudor window frames, picture and dado rails, Potts cabinet clock above a fireplace and some vintage bench seating. Decorated with brewery posters and local historical photos, railway interest is provided by Dewsbury station and signal box signs, a local BR timetable for 1956 and a headboard for *The West Riding* train. Antiques include an engraved glass door panel bearing the name of the 'White Swan' and a 'White Swan' inn sign.

Eight hand-pumps on the central counter have a bias towards beers from the North and Lincolnshire, usually including a mild and an Anglo-Dutch ale, brewed by a local Dutchman. Timothy Taylor (Dark Mild and Landlord), Acorn, Batemans and Black Sheep feature regularly. There is a selection of Belgian bottled beers. A beer list appears on the pub's website. A notice behind the bar announces the number of pints consumed by thirsty customers the previous week (3,010). The menu includes an 'Ale Day Breakfast' on Saturdays plus Sunday roasts. Meals are also available from Monday to Friday lunchtimes and selected evenings. Beer festivals are held twice a year. T-shirts bearing the slogan 'I missed the train at Dewsbury' are on sale. Children welcome until 5pm; occasional live music.

The station: Though much of the building has been demolished and its hexagonal chimney-stacks removed, the remainder was renovated in 2000, and features a Jacobean gable and flat-roofed *port-cochère* (vehicle porch). An integral footbridge is another survivor, rising to a hump in the middle and sporting latticed ironwork and decorative wooden valancing. The booking hall has Tudor-style archways and ticket window. A plaque reveals the Grade II listed station cost £5,597 to build. Both platforms have attractive awnings and spandrels, dating from 1885.

> **The West Riding Licensed Refreshment Rooms,**
> **Platform Two, Dewsbury Station, Wellington Road,**
> **Dewsbury, West Yorkshire WF13 1HF. Tel. 01924**
> **459193. Monday to Friday 11am (Monday from**
> **noon) – 11pm (Friday to midnight),**
> **Saturday 10am – midnight, Sunday 11am – 11pm.**
> **www.imissedthetrain.com**

DOWNHAM MARKET, NORFOLK

Former Great Eastern Railway
between Ely and King's Lynn.

THE RAILWAY ARMS

Stepping from the London-bound platform through the door of this delightful station building is like entering the house of a favourite but slightly eccentric uncle. There is a collection of railway memorabilia, books, photos and even a working model railway, in comfortable surroundings furnished with armchairs, a tiled fireplace and Tiffany wall lamps. Its focal point is a compact corner servery, edged with saw-tooth valancing, festooned with pump-clips and stocked with three carefully chosen ales. If the customer chooses one of these, the server will ignore the hand-pumps, calmly walk away from the bar, weave past fellow customers, and disappear into another room. He (or she) is not being anti-social: this is the tap room, where casks are racked and beer poured by gravity before being delivered to the thirsty recipient via the same circuitous route. One ale is invariably from Cambridgeshire brewery Elgood's (on my visit the hoppy Pageant), others were Nethergate's Suffolk County and Sharp's Doom Bar, plus a draught cider, Crone's.

At the heart of this compact hostelry is a sitting room with a settle and occasional tables, each with a vase of fresh flowers, gathered around the fireplace. Its similarity to country railway waiting rooms of old extends to the reproductions of classic railway posters on the walls. I would have not been surprised if a 1930s-era stationmaster had entered, complete with a carnation in his lapel. Setting it apart from that era, however, are the modern 25Kv A.C. electric trains calling at the platform a few feet away while, inside, an O gauge model train completes a circuit of its high-level track on request. Running just below ceiling height, the model uses 'tunnels' through the walls! Another room is lined with bookcases and doubles as a second-hand bookshop, complete with armchairs to facilitate comfortable browsing, an honesty box being left for sales

Above: *The Railway Arms, which incorporates a secondhand bookshop with armchairs, occupies the far wing of the station building.*
Below: *Note the working model railway running above the bar counter! The hand-pumps are for show: ale is drawn directly from the cask in an adjacent tap-room.*

money. Stained glass panels of medieval English archers lead customers through an archway into the bar and the adjoining Fenland Express Café, serving hot and cold light snacks.

The bar has a loyal local following of which the locals are clearly proud. One regular told me with a grin that he'd recently had to wait here for three hours to meet his partner returning late from London – so had whiled away the time sampling all the beers. There was a steady stream of customers on a Saturday afternoon, the conversation assisted by the absence of background music (the reproduction vintage 'wireless' was turned off.) Bar snacks such as salt beef sandwiches, bacon baps and a cheese board are available Thursday to Saturday evenings. Take away beers available, dogs welcome.

The station and nearby: With its two Dutch gabled pavilions, tall angled chimneys and lozenge-shaped windows, the station dates from 1846 and is Grade II listed. It looks better now than it did in the 1950s, when its front awning was missing and roofing was with corrugated asbestos. In the early 1990s it was re-roofed with hand-made tiles. Construction is of delicate carstone slips (a soft local stone), edged with buff brick, and big iron brackets support the platform awning. There's a matching brick shelter on the down platform, and a weather boarded signal box guards a level crossing (there is no footbridge); an old flour-mill is adjacent. It's a short walk into Downham with its old pubs, Victorian town hall and clock tower. To the south, seen from the train, is Denver Mill, a tower windmill (*circa* 1835), last in the county still working as such, and open to visitors. Denver once had a junction station (for Stoke Ferry).

The Railway Arms, Downham Market Station, Railway Road, Norfolk, PE38 9EN. Tel. 01366 386636. Monday to Thursday 10am – 12.10pm, 3.30 – 5.30 (Thurs. 10.30pm), Friday 10am – 10.30pm, Saturday 10am – noon, 4.30 – 10.30pm, Sunday noon – 2.30pm. www.railway-arms.co.uk

FOXFIELD, CUMBRIA

Former Furness Railway between
Barrow-in-Furness and Whitehaven.

PRINCE OF WALES & FOXFIELD BREWERY

A scenic stretch of the Cumbrian Coast line traces a giant horseshoe around the Duddon Estuary – a haven for birdlife and, less well-known, home to 20 per cent of the nation's natterjack toads. Foxfield Station sits 'mid-horseshoe' where the railway crosses the estuary. Opposite is this pub, once a tied house of Brockbank's Bank Springs Brewery, part of a family run estate which operated until the mid 1950s around Millom. Now a family-run brewpub and freehouse, devoid of lavish decor or grand architecture, yet welcoming and well run. On my first visit I was soon having conversations with staff and fellow drinkers as if I were an old friend. In recent years it has won 'Best Railway Pub' from the Association of Community Rail Partnerships and awards for its ale, cider and perry from CAMRA.

A beer connoisseurs' haven, three of the six hand-pumps were devoted to Foxfield brews on my visit (Pearly Sands, 3.6% ABV, Tim's Brown 3.7% and Cascaded Encounter 4.3%), the

A goods train heading towards Barrow, with Fowler 4F No.44347 in charge, steams through Foxfield on a sunny May day in 1959. The Prince of Wales is on the right.

A slate-built wall and water tower frame this modern view of the Prince of Wales, seen from the station platform.

malts. The impressive selections are listed on two blackboards. The main bar room boasts a veteran bar-billiards table (shove ha'penny is also played) and picture windows giving a view of the signal box and passing trains. There are two coal fires. Railway items include two BR era Foxfield totem station signs (one purchased by a group of pub regulars), a Canadian Pacific Railway mirror and a steam-era photograph of the station when it was a junction.

Local author Ian Davidson worked on the Coniston branch as a porter when a young man and is still a regular at the pub. In his book of reminiscences, *Dynamiting Niagara,* he recalls a colleague, Ab Tyson, who managed to combine the jobs of platelayer and pub landlord (though not at this establishment):

'It's a mortal disease, working on the railway. Yance ye've catched it ye're nivver cured.'

Outdoor paved drinking area with tram-style knifeboard seats. Dogs are welcome; live music on Wednesdays several times a month; beer festivals and other events; bar games. Bed and breakfast (discount for CAMRA members). No food is served; no ambient music; credit cards not accepted.

The station: This was once the junction for the Coniston branch, which closed to passengers in 1958. Though much of the station building and ancillary structures have gone, those remaining are well maintained. There is a stone-built water tower and, on the single island platform, a weather-boarded signal box, still in use. This extends to form an integral passenger waiting shelter and, with a gated level crossing and semaphore signal, makes an attractive scene. It is a request stop and no passenger trains run on Sundays.

remaining ones dispensing interesting micro-brews (Cambrinus Lamp Oil Porter, Acorn Darkness and Salamander Gung-Ho). There is also a good range of foreign bottled beers including examples of Belgian Lambic and Gueuze styles, with others from Germany and the USA, plus real ciders and perries and a range of malt whiskies, including special bottlings and rare

Prince of Wales, Foxfield, near Broughton-in-Furness, Cumbria, LA20 6BX. Tel. 01229 716238.
Wednesday and Thursday, 2.45 – 11pm.
Friday to Sunday, noon – 11pm (Sun. 10.30pm).
Closed Monday and Tuesday.
www.princeofwalesfoxfield.co.uk

GROSMONT, NORTH YORKSHIRE

Former North Eastern Railway between Whitby and Pickering and Middlesbrough. Now terminus of the North Yorkshire Moors Railway (NYMR) a heritage line from Pickering.

THE CROSSING CLUB AND STATION TAVERN

Despite the village's remote location amid the North York Moors National Park, Grosmont Station is quite substantial, with four platforms. The hamlet grew in importance because of the railway: indeed, it was first known as Tunnel after the main permanent way feature. (George Stephenson, fresh from his triumph with the Stockton and Darlington, started work on the Whitby and Pickering line as early as 1833.) It still oozes history, and steam. The two featured hostelries (which are independent of each other) lie either side of a level crossing.

Most unusual, yet easy to miss, is **The Crossing Club**. Its diminutive size belies its riches in the form of micro-brewery beers, railway atmosphere and friendly banter. Its rather anonymous entrance, adjacent to one of the country's smallest Co-operative stores (opened in 1867 and once supplied by railway wagons rolled, via small turntables, directly into the premises) and an even smaller model railway shop, could be mistaken for an office or undertakers. Crossing the threshold, however, the visitor passes a set of mock level crossing gates – complete with red lamps and white picket fencing – and, climbing a few steps, enters a dimly lit, carpeted bar festooned with signal box track diagrams, faded black-and-white steam photos and, affixed to ceiling beams, an array of real ale pump-clips. More than six hundred of them: the number served since the club was set up some ten years ago by enterprising volunteers from the NYMR engine shed to: 'Create and maintain an intimate and convivial atmosphere for members to meet... and a hub to the social life of the village.' There are five hand-pulls on the corner bar counter, with three ales usually available (from Captain Cook, Durham and Bull Lane breweries

on my visit). Non-members are welcome, signing-in on a well-thumbed ledger at the bar. Seating is on benches and stools; while a trip to the toilets involves descent of a steep flight of stairs. Do not expect food: the attractions here are ale and ambience. It doesn't take many customers to make the place seem busy, and it is likely you will overhear terms such as 'coupling rods' and 'valve-gear' in the buzz of conversation. Visitors doing the Rail Ale Trail along the Esk Valley Railway are among the clientele. Take outs are provided for those supplying a container!

The level crossing and signal box at Grosmont, with the Station Tavern, formerly the Tunnel Inn, beyond.

The Station Tavern is much older, a stone-built inn which was clearly of importance as it boasts a Doric porch, pan-tiled roof (rather than slate) and ornate, ogee shaped lintels on ground floor windows. Built around 1835 as Tunnel Inn, and latterly called the Station Hotel, this staging post had stables behind (the roof line of which can be seen from its car park). George Stephenson's railway was initially horse-drawn and a regular service ran between Whitby and 'The Tunnel Inn'. The horse tunnel still exists, one of the first used by passenger trains, now providing pedestrian access to the locomotive shed, base for A4 Pacific *Sir Nigel Gresley*. The bar has three hand-pumps, serving Black Sheep Best Bitter, Camerons Strongarm and John Smith's Cask when I visited. Decoration includes limited edition prints of locomotives, and local historical photos. The menu is varied and served lunchtimes and evenings. It is advisable to start here before moving to the Crossing Club, which doesn't serve food and opens later. Both venues have background music, dartboards, and dogs are welcome. The Tavern has a cavernous family room, a roadside patio (with train views), and offers B&B accommodation.

Nearby: The junction station, affected by Beeching's axe in 1965, is now cast in the mid-1950s era. The Grade II listed station house was built in 1846 by the York and North Midland Railway and features an 1870s clock from Northallerton. The wooden booking office is c.1913, from nearby Sleights, while the brick-built signal box is recent: erected by the NYMR in 1996 using a NER design of 1873-1903. The NYMR is one of the country's longest preserved lines and trains regularly continue on the main-line to Whitby. A stop at Goathland is worthwhile and a walk along the original Stephenson track-bed takes you to the Birch Hall Inn, an unspoilt, riverside real-ale gem, at Beck Hole. You can return to Grosmont on foot, using a three-mile trail along the original 1830s track bed. Goathland doubled as Aidensfield on television's *Heartbeat*, and Hogsmeade in the first *Harry Potter* film. Grosmont is a stop for hikers doing the Coast to Coast walk.

The Crossing Club, Co-operative Building, Front Street, Grosmont, North Yorkshire, YO22 5QE. Tel. 07766 197744. Daily 8 – 11pm (closed Sundays and alternate Mondays in winter).

The Station Tavern, Front Street, Grosmont, North Yorkshire, YO22 5PA. Tel. 01947 895060. Daily, 11.30am – 11pm (except Monday to Friday in winter, when hours are 6.30 – 11.30pm). www.stationtavern-grosmont.co.uk

---

HARTLEPOOL, COUNTY DURHAM

Former North Eastern Railway between Sunderland and Stockton.

THE RAT RACE ALE HOUSE

North East England is the cradle of railways – Stockton, of Stockton & Darlington Railway fame, is just up the line – though this bolt-hole does not have such a long history. On the contrary, it is one of country's first 'micro pubs' and was established by ale enthusiast Peter Morgan in 2009, in the station building of 1880. The premises, previously used as a taxi office and newsagents, measures just 20 by 14 feet. There is no counter: instead, a partitioned inner sanctum serves as a cellar, where casks are kept cool and from which beer is drawn directly.

Four changing ales from independent breweries are indicated on a blackboard, which also shows an 'L' against the suggested beer for lager, or 'learner' real ale drinkers. Beer is either hand-pulled or drawn directly from the cask (customers can choose). Two from Bath Brewery, along with one from Manchester micro-brewer Marble, and 2004 CAMRA British champion Kelham Island Pale Rider, were available on my visit. Traditional cider, wine and soft drinks are also served, and jugs of beer and take-aways can be provided, with disposable glasses if required. Meals are not served, though customers are welcome to bring their own.

There is a friendly atmosphere, with games such as cards and dominoes played and Peter acting as 'mine host'. Seating is on vintage stools and church pews that were obtained from e-Bay. Games, a small library of books (for sale) and newspapers are provided. Railway art prints by Belgian artist Paul Delvaux are displayed, with a growing collection of pump-clips. Toilets are separate, near the ticket office (key available for disabled toilet). Access from street and platform is level.

The station, formerly West Hartlepool, was rationalized in the 1960s and became run-down but was renovated in time for the 2010 Tall Ships Race. The main building, of red brick, has a wooden canopy on the roadside entrance. The platform (there

The Rat Race sells an ever changing range of real ale but doesn't stock lager and has no bar counter.

is only one, as the old northbound platform is no longer used) is covered with a new glazed awning supported on early decorative spandrels with cast-iron brackets incorporating NER monograms. A ceramic tiled route map of the old NER is adjacent to the pub.

Nearby: The Hartlepool Dock and Railway Company created extensive docks here and opened a new line in the early 1850s. The 'new' town of West Hartlepool, masterminded by Ward Jackson, soon dwarfed the original town. The Historic Quay, with its restored buildings and the warship HMS *Trincomalee,* is within walking distance. Trains from the south cross Yarm Viaduct, dating from 1849, half-a-mile in length and with 43 arches, a mighty monument to the railway age. *Daily Mirror* cartoon character (and pub goer) Andy Capp, and his creator Reg Smythe, were both locals.

The Rat Race Ale House, Station Road, Hartlepool, TS24 7ED. Tel. 07903 479378. Tuesday to Friday 12.02 – 2.15pm and 4.02 – 8.15pm, Saturday 12.02 – 9pm *(sic)*. Closed Sunday and Monday. www.ratracealehouse.co.uk

HELWITH BRIDGE (nearest station Horton-in-Ribblesdale), NORTH YORKSHIRE

Former Midland Railway main line between Settle and Appleby.

THE HELWITH BRIDGE

Once a place of refreshment for railway navvies and filled with memorabilia, this stone-built hostelry is hard by the bridge from which it takes its name. This straddles both the River Ribble and the Settle to Carlisle line, with the distinctive peak of Pen-y-ghent as a backdrop. The tracks are yards from the inn's walls and a special outdoor 'lookout' is provided for those who want to watch the freight trains and steam specials. The core of the pub dates from *circa* 1820, when it started life as the canteen for Helwith Bridge Quarry, with the kitchen in the cellar. By the time the Midland started its superbly engineered line to Scotland in the 1870s, it had been enlarged and transformed into a public house, ideally placed to serve the influx of navvies who swelled the population. Being an inn-keeper was lucrative in those days but could be risky. Hard-drinking navvies were prone to fights and rowdiness – court records show a licensee at Langcliffe, to the south, was murdered by one.

A slate floor, rough-hewn stone fireplace, wood panelling, low ceiling and settle-type seating in the main room (there are three others, including one with a pool table and dartboard) combine to give a rustic atmosphere. With a coal fire blazing, this is a comfortable place in which to sit out a Dales blizzard, of which it has seen many. Artefacts reflect landlord Colin Hall's life-long rail enthusiasm. An ardent trainspotter in his youth, he has held the pub for 12 years and, when I rang him, he had just watched LMS Jubilee class *Leander* speed past on a special. Photographs include another special blasting across Ribblehead Viaduct in 1986 and a Stanier Pacific passing the inn with the Royal Train; there are prints of the 'Waverley Express' crossing Arten Gill viaduct, and a large Cuneo reproduction of record-breaking Pacific *Mallard*. Two replica train headboards, the 'Waverley' and 'Thames-Clyde

Express', also have pride of place.

Eight hand-pumps serve a house bitter from Settle-based Three Peaks Brewery and changing guest ales. On my visit they were Hop Back Summer Lightning, Brains Up and Over, Mild Mayhem and Deuchars IPA, the last two from Caledonian. Regulars are Caledonian 80/-, John Smiths and Charles Wells Bombardier.

Ramblers, cavers, rail enthusiasts and locals mingle amiably in this remote, friendly establishment. Apart from the occasions when Colin turns his talents to being the house DJ, there is no music. A snack menu is served at lunchtime with a more varied menu, including vegetarian options, from Thursday to Saturday evenings (also Saturday lunchtime) and on Sunday afternoon. Children allowed until 9pm; dogs welcome. Camping, and bunkhouse accommodation (amusingly named Hotel Paradiso) is available. The nearest station is two miles north. I made the easy riverside walk one sunny morning, leaving a train load of well-equipped walkers to tackle a far more challenging hike.

> **The Helwith Bridge, near Horton-in-Ribblesdale, North Yorkshire, BD24 0EH. Tel. 01729 860220. Daily 2.30pm – midnight (Friday to Sunday from noon). www.helwithbridge.com**

The Helwith Bridge, with Settle & Carlisle tracks in the foreground and the pub's train watchers' lookout on the right-hand side.

HORSTED KEYNES, WEST SUSSEX

Former London Brighton & South Coast Railway, now the Bluebell Railway, a heritage line between Sheffield Park and Kingscote (extension to East Grinstead under construction).

GEORGE V REFRESHMENT ROOM AND RAIL ALE TRAIN

Built in 1882 in the Queen Anne style and now restored to represent a country junction station in 1935, Horsted Keynes is a gem beloved by producers of period television dramas. Buildings are resplendent in Southern Railway green-and-cream, the staff clothed in SR uniforms and piles of time-worn suitcases await shipment on the platform. The George V Refreshment Room, named in honour of the king who celebrated 25 years on the throne and his 70th birthday in 1935, is a narrow, island platform hostelry with a wood-panelled interior. Three antique hand-pulls on the polished wooden bar counter, a mirrored bar back, SR wall clock, stained glass windows and *faux* oil lamps combine with the sound and smell of steam engines to create a setting that exercises all the senses.

The attention to detail extends to vintage signs, posters for the 'Golden Arrow' Pullman train, and a neat row of antique beer bottles, including some from long vanished Lewes brewer Beard & Co.; while vintage cigarette packets such as Woodbine, Craven 'A' and Player's Navy Cut and Weights are displayed as if awaiting purchase. Only an ice-cream refrigerator and glass-fronted food warmer bring the visitor abruptly back to the twenty-first century. On my visit, during one of the Rail Ale events described below, the hand-pulls were being used to serve the crisp, hoppy Windblower from Dudley brewer Holdens, White Horse Saracen from Oxfordshire and Hammerpot Vinery Mild, brewed once a year. Ale is normally confined to bottled versions except during special events and peak periods, so it's wise to check in advance. A small range of hot and cold snacks is served.

Far from being a sleepy place during the pre-preservation

The George V Refreshment Room.

era, the refreshment room was frequently busier than pubs in the nearby village (much to the chagrin of local landlords). Weekend ramblers' excursions, run by the railway from the early 1930s until car ownership became common, returned to London from here. Crowds of hikers would pile in, anxious for a drink before heading home. Similarly, there was a brisk trade when the local hunt met on Sundays. More recently, poet Sir John Betjeman used the bar for the opening sequence in his acclaimed 1972 **BBC** documentary *Metro-Land*.

It is worth synchronising a visit to the Bluebell Railway with a ride on its **Rail Ale Train**. Steam-hauled (as are all passenger trains on the line), this carries three barrels of perfectly conditioned ale to quench the thirst of several dozen thirsty train and beer fans, and provides two refreshment stops en route, at Sheffield Park and Horsted Keynes. I joined the train one bright spring evening with a group of friends, the scent of blossom hanging in the country air, as the sun cast long, willowy shadows across the platform. At the head of a rake of Mark I carriages was Southern tank engine No. B473, resplendent in its olive green livery. Though there was a

Southern Region buffet car in the consist, this wasn't the real ale bar, which was set up instead in a brake second corridor coach (BSK). This contained two trestle tables supporting the casks, charged with ales from Bexhill-on-Sea brewer White. As we travelled the nine-mile line (soon to be eleven), volunteers came to chat with passengers about the railway and the Rail Ale Train, explaining that it began in 2008 and focuses on a different local brewer each time. And that a newly married couple had recently used the train for their wedding breakfast.

On arrival at Sheffield Park, passengers disembarked for a pasty and chip supper (a vegetarian option must be pre-ordered) and the option of two more ales in the rather canteen-like Bessemer Arms, named after the local resident who first saved the line from closure. The highlight, though, was a prolonged stop at Horsted Keynes, where a jazz band struck up on the platform as steam rose up between the carriages and an orange glow from the firebox lit the footplate. Passengers can wander around with their beers, purchased either on the train or in the Refreshment Room. Tours of the Carriage and Wagon Works were an unexpected highlight, a rare chance to see how antique

Happy bar volunteers in the Mark I BSK coach on the Rail Ale Train of 16 April, 2010. LBSCR 0-6-2 tank No. B473 was providing haulage.

items of rolling stock, often discovered decaying on farms and in gardens, are painstakingly returned to their former glory. The Rail Ale train provides an unhurried, informal evening on a delightful pre-1955 period branch line: the first standard gauge one in preservation. There was an efficient bus connection to and from the main line at East Grinstead and the ticket included vouchers for a hot meal and the first pint.

> **George V Refreshment Room, Platforms Three/Four, Horsted Keynes Station, Horsted Keynes, West Sussex, RH17 7BB. Tel. 01825 720801 during office hours. Usually open 11am – 4pm when 'service one' timetable is operating (no evenings except for special events). The Rail Ale Train runs up to three evenings a year; advance booking essential. Tel. 01825 720800. www.bluebell-railway.co.uk**

The Head of Steam occupies the former Lancashire & Yorkshire Railway's wing of a station often described as a 'stately home for trains'.

HUDDERSFIELD, WEST YORKSHIRE (1)

Former London & North Western and Lancashire & Yorkshire Joint, between Leeds and Manchester and terminus of the Penistone line from Sheffield.

THE HEAD OF STEAM

Huddersfield is not only one of Britain's most handsome stations and one that offers a choice of scenic rail routes across Yorkshire and the Pennines, but also one of the few to boast two historical pubs. The Head of Steam, situated in the former Lancashire & Yorkshire Railway's west wing of the imposing frontage (note the L&Y insignia above the entrance), is one of the chain of free houses set up by Tony Brookes in the mid-'90s. After years of dereliction, the building was renovated and opened in spring 1996. Enter via the front with its stone columns, or from the platform beneath the train-shed roof: by either route you have found an Aladdin's Cave, a cross between a museum, an art gallery, a model shop and an eccentric

collector's front room. There are five rooms to be precise, each different in theme and character, around a central servery.

A collection of memorabilia, claimed to be second only in size to that of the National Railway Museum in the North of England, includes train, engine and station nameplates, assorted signs, posters, maps, photographs and historical track diagrams, plus model trains and buses for sale. A five-inch scale live steam model of a GWR 14xx class tank engine and autocoach have pride of place behind one of the bars. A rear bar has a collection of neon drinks signs and old fashioned enamel advertisements, also a three-dimensional artwork, depicting Huddersfield Station, called *The Geometry of Waiting* by Ali White. Steam railway prints by Arthur E. Gills, a former railwayman, also deck the walls and many are for sale. The crest of West Ham FC is placed in all his paintings. Even the corridor to the toilets has its share of pictures, posters and signs and there's a room devoted to pub games.

There are 12 hand-pumps, divided between three bar counters, and the policy is to serve ales from independent north country breweries. A typical line-up includes examples from

The tram tracks and horse-drawn gigs have gone, but otherwise Huddersfield Station has changed remarkably little since this turn-of-the-century postcard. The left-hand wing is now the Head of Steam.

Black Sheep, Summer Wine, Coach House, Hawkshead, Thwaites (Dark Mild), Samuel Smith, Glentworth and Brass Monkey (Capuchin). There is also a perry and real cider (Weston's Stowford Press). Meals are served daily until mid-evening (Sunday 6pm). Weekly live jazz and blues music. Outside seating and level access from the platform.

The station: Widely regarded as Britain's finest classical station, Grade I listed Huddersfield has been described as a 'stately home for trains' and is set in St George's Square, surrounded by complementary buildings. Dominated by a portico reminiscent of the long lost Euston Arch, the stone building, by the grandly named James Pigott Pritchett, was completed in 1850. The perfectly proportioned frontage is more than 400 feet long. Surveying the scene is a statue of the town's most famous son – Prime Minister Harold Wilson – surrounded by fountains. The pubs are housed in pavilions at either end of the station, which once included separate ticket offices of the London & North Western and Lancashire & Yorkshire Railways, both of which served the town. How many passengers, one wonders, missed their trains by attending the wrong booking office?

The platforms, decorated with Victorian-style lamps, are sheltered by a glazed train-shed. It is not the original but the third on the site: a first replacement collapsed in 1884, killing three men: the one *in situ* dates from 1886.

The Head of Steam, Huddersfield Station, St George's Square, West Yorkshire, HD1 1JB. Tel. 01484 454533. Weekdays 11am – 12.30 am (Friday and Saturday 2am), Sunday noon – 10.30pm. www.theheadofsteam.com

HUDDERSFIELD, WEST YORKSHIRE (2)

THE KING'S HEAD

Occupying the east wing of the station, this establishment was first licensed in the 1890s, when it served as the first class refreshment room for the Huddersfield & Manchester Railway. The company's crest is still above the frontage overlooking St George's Square. An original, mosaic tiled floor and marble fireplaces, now fitted with solid fuel stoves, give a hint to past opulence, though the high ceiling has long been obscured by a false one. The landlord would like to remove this and restore the room to its former glory.

The pub's main feature is this large room with bar at one end, ideally suited to live music, performed several times weekly. There are smaller rooms to each side, reached through open archways. A blackboard details ales on offer from the ten hand-pumps. On my last visit these were from Timothy Taylor's, Oakham, Dark Star, Bobs, Bradfield, Boggart (mild), Green Mill, Greenfield (Retro Rail Ale) and Northern (a chocolate stout). Several awards have been bestowed by the local CAMRA branch. No meals served, sandwiches available. There are monthly 'Railway Nights' with slides and DVDs shown. Children and dogs welcome. Background music. There is level access from the platform side.

TRANS-PENNINE ALE TRAIL AND MUSIC TRAINS

Huddersfield, straddling three deep valleys in the Pennine Hills, is a junction on the Trans-Pennine line with frequent services linking Newcastle, York, Manchester and Liverpool. The views are first-class as the trains sweep over majestic viaducts and through tunnels, which open up to panoramic vistas of stone-built towns and villages. If possible, admire the slender viaducts around Huddersfield from afar, notably 120ft-high Lockwood Viaduct which is contemporary with the station. At Marsden is Standege Tunnel, one of Britain's longest, at three miles, and reputedly haunted. There are walks along the canal between Marsden and Huddersfield, so you can work up a thirst, returning by train from Slaithwaite if required.

Aware that some good pubs are as much a feature of their route as the scenery, the railway company helps promote a Trans-Pennine Real Ale Trail linking the pubs (www.realaletrail.net). Running south from Huddersfield is the Penistone line, another scenic route through the West Riding to Barnsley and Sheffield. Twenty-nine-arch Penistone Viaduct is one of the highlights. Previously threatened with closure, the line is supported by the local community – known as a Community Rail Partnership – and one of its novel features is the occasional Music Train. Scheduled services become mobile entertainment venues, with on-board musicians entertaining passengers, who pay the normal fares. The trains are often themed to special occasions, such as Yorkshire Day or Hallowe'en and are a novel way of travelling the line.

The King's Head, Huddersfield Station, St George's Square, West Yorkshire, HD1 1JF. Tel. 01484 511058.
Monday to Saturday 11.30am – 11pm,
Sunday, noon – 10.30pm.
www.the-kings-head-huddersfield.co.uk

KEIGHLEY, WEST YORKSHIRE

Former Midland Railway between Leeds and Skipton, also terminus of the Keighley & Worth Valley Railway, a heritage line to Oxenhope.

REAL ALE BUFFET CAR

It is rare to be able to drink real ale on a scheduled steam-hauled train, particularly one with a properly equipped British Railways Mark I Buffet Car (RMB). This one has featured in the indispensable aid for ale drinkers, CAMRA's *Good Beer Guide*. It travels the line used for the 1970 film version of *The Railway Children*, starring Jenny Agutter and Bernard Cribbins, which gives the K&WVR a special place in people's affections.

I travelled on Yorkshire Day (1 August), so there was a jovial atmosphere on board. The ebullient female ticket collector was wearing a white rose on her lapel and there was a discussion about famous Yorkshire folk. The Buffet Car sports picture windows, below which are Formica covered tables and high-back upholstered seats. A section of the car sports the immaculately-kept bar, with three hand-pumps. Three local ales are usually available, though only two on my journey: Timothy Taylor Bitter and Skipton Copper Dragon. The bar back is lined, pub-style, with a selection of spirits optics, and bottles of beer, wine and soft drinks. Tea and coffee are available, as are confectionery and sandwiches.

What is the secret to storing and serving real ale on a

This Mark I RMB Buffet Car on the Keighley & Worth Valley Railway, seen here in August 2005, is equipped with three working hand-pumps.

moving train, surely not conducive to the storage of casks that require a period of settlement before use? The trick is that, before the journey, conditioned beer is decanted from casks into containers resembling stainless steel tea urns that are carried aboard. It may not be very scientific but it works. The railway goes five miles into Brontë country, the steam engine storming up a gradient out of Keighley, past reminders of the many woollen mills which once dotted the area. The sights and sounds are superb and the beer, delicious. The only way to better it would be to come back and do the same at the railway's annual Beer and Music festival in October.

Nearby: The K&WVR is an atmospheric way of reaching a literary shrine: the Brontë Parsonage at Haworth, a short walk from the station. Keighley has a good selection of real ale pubs for its size, including the Boltmakers Arms (effectively the brewery tap for Timothy Taylor) and the Brown Cow, both CAMRA award winners.

Real Ale Bar & Buffet Car, c/o Keighley & Worth Valley Railway, The Railway Station, Haworth, Keighley, West Yorkshire BD22 8NJ. Tel. 01535 645214 (office hours). The Buffet Car is usually carried on 'main service' steam trains (including weekends and daily during school holidays). www.kwvr.co.uk

KIDDERMINSTER TOWN, WORCESTERSHIRE

Terminus of the Severn Valley Railway (formerly GWR) a heritage line to Bridgnorth. Adjacent to main line station on former GWR Birmingham to Worcester line.

KING AND CASTLE

This spacious Great Western Railway 1930s-style refreshment room is set in a building that looks every inch a nineteenth century GWR terminus but is in fact a reproduction created in the twentieth. A GWR monogrammed carpet, and varnished tables and chairs set in two neat lines, give a formal look to the large room, with its bar at one end and fireplace at the other. The atmosphere is the opposite: informal, with talk of Black Fives, footplate experiences, Crewe in steam days and the merits of local breweries often to be heard. Six hand-pumps furnish the marble-topped bar counter, serving ales from the area. Wyre Piddle's Royal Piddle is the house bitter, accompanied by Bathams Bitter and Hobsons (Mild), with Holdens Windblower, Potton Shambles and Excelsior Golden Ale as guests on my visit, plus two ciders from Kingstone.

Opened in 1986 on the former goods yard site, a few yards from the modern main line station, Kidderminster Town is based on an 1890 design for Ross-on-Wye. It has a glazed canopy over the concourse, its steelwork based on Wolverhampton Low Level. Entrance to the pub, via the cobbled station approach, is heralded by a working gas lamp (one of many examples on the station) and a GWR black-and-white wooden sign bearing its name. The interior, with its neatly upholstered bench seating, features details such as period ceiling roses, coving and picture rails. Even the toilet doors carry chocolate-and-cream cast-iron signs. Decoration includes a series of black-and-white images depicting the GWR's multi-faceted operations, from dining cars to road services, from expresses such as the 'Cheltenham Flyer' to a photo-call of Kings and Castles newly built at Swindon. Above the fireplace, with its wood fire, is a railway poster of the capital, captioned 'London Pride,' a wall clock with GWR roundel providing the finishing touch. Cobs are sold at the bar but meals and snacks are served in an adjacent dining room (not evenings). Children and dogs are welcome. To take a drink on the train, ask for a disposable glass.

The King and Castle, Kidderminster Town Station, Comberton Hill, Kidderminster, Worcestershire, DY10 1QX. Tel. 01562 747505. Monday to Saturday 11am – 11pm, Sunday noon – 10.30pm. www.svr.co.uk

The King & Castle.

Brief Encounter, in its classic Midland Railway station building.

LANGWATHBY, CUMBRIA

Former Midland Railway between
Appleby and Carlisle.

BRIEF ENCOUNTER (LICENSED, NO REAL ALE)

A cosy tea-shop and café, with pink table-cloths and rustic fireplace, occupies the former booking hall of this restored station, built in Derby Gothic style in 1876 and set in the pastoral Eden Valley. The ladies' waiting room is now the kitchen. Home-made jam and cakes; local ice-cream. The old goods shed survives nearby while the former stationmaster's house is on the right as you come up the drive.

Brief Encounter Café Restaurant, Langwathby Station, Langwathby, Penrith, Cumbria, CA10 1NB. Tel. 01768 881902. Daily (March – October) 9am – 5pm. Tuesday to Sunday (October to December) 10am – 4pm. Closed January and February. www.briefencounterlangwathby.co.uk

LEITH CENTRAL, EDINBURGH
(station closed)

Terminus of North British Railway branch from Edinburgh (Waverley).

CENTRAL BAR (NO REAL ALE)

This is one of the most ornate watering holes in Scotland. The station it served, closed more than half-a-century ago, was vast. With a 220ft-wide single-span roof visible from a mile away, this railway 'cathedral' was only in passenger use from 1903-52 and the roof was demolished in the eighties. A clock-turreted corner entrance survives, along with an Italian Renaissance station frontage, behind which sits – like a pearl in an oyster – the Category B listed Central Bar.

The bar, which pre-dates the railway's opening by a few years, was designed by prolific Edinburgh pub architect P.L. Henderson and employs every device in his armoury. Floor-to-ceiling tiling by Minton Hollins; carved oak features including a U-shaped bar and fire surround; tall mirrors; a Jacobean papier-mâché ceiling; mosaic-tiled porches and windows of stained and leaded glass. Tiling incorporates four large panels of Scottish sporting scenes: golfing, sailing, hare-coursing and grouse shooting are depicted. Behind the counter is an ornate oak-carved gantry (bar-back) featuring four menacing-looking griffins. Seating along one wall takes the form of four U-shaped, upholstered benches and tables set on fancy cast-iron legs. The name of the first owner, John Doig, is immortalised in coloured glass panels and some decorative casks.

Leith-born author Irvine Welsh set some of his novel *Trainspotting* in this establishment, as one of hard-man Begbie's haunts. Let that not concern you: though it *is* a male-oriented bar with some distractions, such as television and background music, the atmosphere is friendly. No food is served but, in the absence of real ale, the Belhaven Best is a refreshing pint.

Nearby: The four-track railway and platforms, elevated 15 feet above road level, are long gone, as is the 81-lever signal

GNSR 4-4-0 No.49 Gordon Highlander *with a 'Scottish Rambler' excursion at Leith Central in April 1965, showing the station's vast train-shed.*

The Central Bar in 2006.

box. They were razed to be replaced by a supermarket and 'Waterworld'. Leith was (and is) the port of Edinburgh, linked to Princes Street via the once fashionable Leith Walk and served by frequent buses. A short distance beyond is Ocean Terminal where the former Royal Yacht *Britannia,* built on Clydebank in 1952, is permanently berthed, now a tourist attraction.

Central Bar, 7-9 Leith Walk, Leith, EH6 8LN. Tel. 0131 555 2006. Weekdays 9am – midnight (Friday and Saturday 1am), Sunday 12.30pm – midnight.

LUDLOW, SHROPSHIRE

Former Shrewsbury & Hereford Railway (LNWR and GWR joint) between Hereford and Shrewsbury.

LUDLOW BREWING COMPANY

A large goods shed north of the station has been given a new lease of life as a working brewery. A licensed bar enables visitors to drink where wagons were once loaded and unloaded, surrounded by the sights, sounds and aromas of beer production. The railway arrived in 1852-3 and this became a busy place. Coal, timber, grain, other foodstuffs and cattle were handled in large quantities but everything fell silent in 1968 when the goods yard was closed (the old station building was demolished around the same time). The brick-built shed, used variously as builders' merchants and a commercial vehicle garage, fell into a semi-derelict state. At one stage demolition was threatened. The good folk of Ludlow Brewery, who started in 2006 in an old maltsters' building on the same site (the street was full of maltings until the 1930s), needed to expand and saw salvation across the yard. They lodged a planning application in 2009 and the shed's conversion to a 20-barrel capacity brewery, complete with Brewery Tap

and visitor facilities, began the same year. Completed in 2011, visitors can quaff samples of all the company's ales, including its very first brew, Gold and the full-bodied Black Knight Stout, at a brick-built servery. There is a spacious 'auditorium', with seating both at ground and mezzanine level, the latter giving a bird's eye view of the brewing equipment. There are guided tours (booking advised) but the Tap operates like a pub, albeit with shorter hours, and occasional evenings of live music.

Additions to the original building include a slate floor with low-energy underfloor heating, a railway-style canopy over the entrance and a low extension parallel to the main-line, housing temperature-controlled beer stillage and toilets. The wooden roof trusses and slate tiling have been restored.

Nearby: Ludlow, with its castle and half-timbered buildings, is a delight to explore and its Food Festival, staged in September, held in high regard. The Marches Line, following the England/Wales border through a pretty landscape of pastoral farmland, hills and meandering rivers, is recommended. Semaphore signalling remains in several places, while Abergavenny Station has its Whistle Stop Café. Ludlow's has a privately run Travel Centre opened in 2002.

Ludlow Brewing Company Ltd, Kingsley Garage, 105 Corve Street, Ludlow, Shropshire SY8 1DJ. Tel. 01584 873291. (Turn right out of station then first right.) Monday to Friday 10am – 5pm, Saturday 10am – 4pm, Sunday closed. www.theludlowbrewingcompany.co.uk

The goods shed at Ludlow, now home to a brewery and bar, as diesel unit 175 116 passes with a Manchester to Milford Haven service in February, 2011.

MANCHESTER (VICTORIA)

Former Manchester & Leeds Railway (later Lancashire & Yorkshire) between Liverpool and Leeds and other destinations (also Metrolink).

METRO BAR (NO REAL ALE)

This Art Nouveau gem dating from 1909 sits under-used and undervalued beside the concourse of one of the country's most historic stations. With a smartly tiled exterior, its former role as First Class Refreshment Room picked out in gilt mosaic letters, and an interior whose highlight is a magnificent dome of coloured glass, it is easy to picture smartly dressed Edwardian travellers enjoying afternoon tea. The walls are set with pastel green tiles decorated with delicate motifs; ceiling edges are finished with plasterwork fruits and flowers and there are marble floors. The former serving hatches are still in evidence and there are entrance lobbies of mosaic tiling and carved wood. Today's food and drink offering is fairly underwhelming, being

A leaded glass dome, surrounded by decorative plasterwork, is highlight of the former Lancashire & Yorkshire Railway's First Class Refreshment Room at Manchester Victoria.

Left: *Manchester Victoria's gem in its original guise as the Grill Room and Restaurant, in 1909. The telegraphic address was 'Stimulant'!*

GRILL ROOM & RESTAURANT, RIA STATION, MANCHESTER.

Telephone: 6178
Telegrams: "Stimulant"

a selection of keg beers and lagers served from a contemporary bar counter, with an adjacent snack bar providing light meals and hot drinks. 'Outside' seating is available on the concourse.

Adjacent is the ground floor remnant (with upper floor added later) of the original Manchester & Leeds station of 1844. The *Manchester Guardian* of 19 August, 1843 claimed that Hunt's Bank, as it was called at first, would be the largest station in the country. Also here is a wood-panelled booking office, still operational, and a large, white-tiled map of the L&Y network. In 2010, Network Rail announced that Manchester Victoria would undergo a £25 million renovation between

2012-14, to include a bright, new roof and that 'heritage features' of the station, such as those in the refreshment room, and the mosaics, would be 'protected'. There is hope that this remarkable but faded place will bloom once again.

Nearby: The Museum of Science and Industry in Manchester, in Liverpool Road, is partly set in the world's oldest surviving railway station, the original and first terminus of the Liverpool & Manchester Railway until its extension to Victoria. Manchester-built locomotives, including a powerful Beyer-Garratt, form part of the collection and there are vintage steam rides at weekends.

> Metro Bar, Manchester Victoria Station,
> Manchester M3 1NY. Tel. 0161 835 9586.
> Monday to Thursday 7am – 11pm, Friday and
> Saturday 7am – midnight, Sunday 9am – 10pm.

MANNINGTREE, ESSEX

Former Great Eastern Railway on main line between Colchester and Ipswich and junction for Harwich.

STATION BUFFET

In the 1640s, Manningtree was centre for the activities of Matthew Hopkins, the Witchfinder General, who conducted a reign of terror hunting down and sentencing to death a score of local 'witches'. Today, thankfully, it is altogether more benign. Until 2004, its refreshment room, on the London platform, had a place on CAMRA's National Inventory of Historic Pub Interiors, along with Bridlington and Stalybridge, as its bar fittings were unchanged since the 1930s. Early that year it was discovered that a refurbishment meant it no longer met the Pub Heritage Group's strict criteria. Nevertheless, the buffet's uncluttered layout and combination of real ale, snacks and hot food (the latter served until at least 1pm) is a place close to the affections of many. It boasts an outside seating area, perfect for train watching. The station building, constructed by the GER at the turn of the twentieth century, is in a semi-rural location so you can also gaze across the fields and reed-lined riverbanks of Constable Country.

There are three hand-pulls, with Greene King IPA and Old Speckled Hen being regulars and the other serving Abbot Ale on my visit.

Nearby: Manningtree has been described as the smallest town in England and its largest village. To the north-west is Dedham Vale, with its wide skies and attractive countryside and villages, where landscape painter John Constable grew up. A footpath from the station leads toward Flatford Mill, East Bergholt and Dedham, all subjects of his canvases.

> Station Buffet, Manningtree Station, Lawford, Essex,
> CO11 2LH. Tel. 01206 391114.
> Monday to Friday 5am – 9pm (Fri. 11pm),
> Saturday 8am – 11pm, Sunday 8am – 2pm.

NEWCASTLE CENTRAL, TYNE & WEAR

Former York, Newcastle & Berwick Railway (NER) on East Coast main line from London (King's Cross) to Edinburgh (Waverley) and other routes.

THE CENTURION BAR

This former First Class Refreshment Room, created in 1893 and Grade I listed, is breathtaking. An orgy of nineteenth century ceramics, mirrors, murals and dark varnished woodwork, the 'room' is the size of a church hall, clad from floor to ceiling in richly coloured ceramic tiles. The tiling – claimed to be worth £3.8 million at today's prices — continues over the ceiling, up to a lantern-style glazed roof. Subtly lit by background lighting which slowly changes colour, this is an atmospheric destination bar and one of the most impressive in a city which has no shortage of good watering holes.

The former First Class Refreshment Room, now the Centurion Bar, at Newcastle Central in 2004.

A Northumbrian mural is framed by fully tiled Corinthian pillars, at the Centurion Bar.

At one end of the room is a mural of idyllic Northumbrian countryside framed by two Corinthian pillars. The central area is set with low tables and poufs, with upholstered seating around the walls. The height of the room is such that it includes an internal balcony, now used for DJ performances. Entertainment is a feature, with live music and DJs several times a week; at other times the volume of background music can be quite high (there is a smaller, quieter bar to the rear). There is a big screen showing major sporting events. Real ales sampled on my visit were from the Captain Cook, Jarrow and Black Sheep breweries. Meals are served until early evening. There is an adjoining deli, with seating in a glass conservatory and 'outside' on the station concourse. Though sadly neglected during British Rail days (at one stage part of the venue was reputedly used as cells by British Transport Police) this jewel in the station's crown was restored by Keeping Inns around the turn of this century.

The station: North East England gave railways to the world and, in return, the railways built one of the country's most opulent stations, dating from 1850. The railway enters the city in triumphant fashion, crossing the Tyne on high bridges, vaulting the city buildings and slicing through the remains of the castle. Such an intervention today would cause an outcry among conservationists! The architect was John Dobson, a prolific worker who could probably have designed a stately home on his day off. This is his finest work, for which he borrowed the style of ancient Rome, using dozens of classical columns – made from iron rather than stone – to support the curving glass roof. There are three acres roofed in glass and timber which, with the sharp curve of the platforms, adds to the elegance. The frontage has Doric columns set either side of nine tall arches.

The Centurion Bar, south end of concourse, Newcastle Central Station, Neville Street, NE1 5DG. Tel. 0191 261 6611. Daily 10am – midnight (Sunday 10.30pm). www.centurion-newcastle.co.uk/bar.asp

NEWTON ST CYRES, DEVON

Former Exeter & Crediton Railway (later LSWR) between Exeter and Barnstaple.

THE BEER ENGINE

This smart brewpub – it is home to a 25 year-old micro-brewery, the oldest in Devon – started life, *circa* 1850, as a railway hotel. The adjacent station is now a single platform request stop where intending passengers must give a hand signal to the driver. A railway theme runs through the pub, from the humorous inn sign depicting an antiquated and overmanned 'brewery on rails', to the equally amusing wall prints by local artist David Johnson. Rail Ale, Piston and Sleeper Heavy, from the brewery on view downstairs, were available on draught when I visited (see page 126); there is also at least one real cider. Take-aways can be supplied!

With its polished wooden floor, brick-faced bar counter and blazing fire, the L-shaped, split-level room is spacious. Clusters of hops hang from the ceiling. Customers range from students to locals and hikers (in fact it was members of the Ramblers who first alerted me to this gem). There is a varied menu using local

The Beer Engine, home to Devon's oldest micro-brewery, was once the station hotel.

ingredients – fish is delivered daily from Brixham. Meals are served daily at lunchtime and in the evening. No ambient music. Outside, an ivy-clad patio and upstairs terrace overlooks the single-track Tarka Line, named after *Tarka the Otter* by local writer Henry Williamson. The route has one of the longest established 'ale trails' – pubs which can be visited by train. As trains are infrequent, it may be more convenient to return to Exeter using a bus which stops on the A377 road, a half-mile walk. See also: Crediton.

Nearby: The Great Western Hotel, next to Exeter St David's Station, has a bar decorated with GWR photos and railway prints. It is also popular with real ale enthusiasts as it normally has nine ales on hand-pump, winning the local CAMRA Pub of the Year Award several times.

> **The Beer Engine, Newton St Cyres, near Exeter, Devon EX5 5AX. Tel. 01392 851282. Monday to Saturday 11am – 11pm, Sunday noon – 10.30pm. www.thebeerengine.co.uk**

OAKHAM, RUTLAND

Former Syston & Peterborough Railway (MR) between Peterborough and Syston (served by Birmingham to Stansted Airport trains).

THE GRAINSTORE BREWERY TAP

A three-storey, nineteenth century railway grain store and goods shed adjacent to this handsome station is home to a brewery whose ales have won many awards. Unlike some conversions, the owners have overlaid their new use very sensitively on the old, so you feel you are stepping back in time. Heavy floor boards and beams, cast-iron columns, bare brick walls and oak barrels – plus intriguing clunking sounds emanating from the upstairs brewery and those of trains going by – contribute to the atmosphere. The annual August beer festival was just setting up in a marquee

The Grainstore Brewery Tap in 2007.

outside as I arrived. Inside, a barmaid was polishing the hand-pumps with Brasso: at 11am on a weekday, business was slack (a rare event at this popular hostelry).

Renovation of the long derelict building began in 1995 and many layers of whitewash and dirt had to be blasted away to reveal the original interior stone and brickwork. The 15 barrel plant opened later that year. It is run like a traditional tower brew house, with raw materials being taken to the top and the finished product emerging from (and dispensed) at the bottom, aided by gravity. A brick-built counter takes up much of one side of the open-plan 'beer hall', set with sturdy wooden tables and chairs. The walls display a compendium of photos, beer mats, CAMRA awards, a letter from HRH The Prince of Wales after his visit and

posters for bands who have performed at the regular live music nights. Four Grainstore ales were available, ranging in strength from Rutland Panther, a mild at 3.4% ABV to Ten Fifty, hoppy and mahogany coloured at 5.0% ABV, plus a guest. Sometimes the choice rises to seven. Meals are served only at lunchtime, ranging from soups and jacket potatoes to sausages with Stilton mash and burgers. Darts and other traditional games are played, and dogs are welcome. Outside is a covered paved area with benches. Guided tours of the brewery should be booked in advance (minimum six persons).

The adjacent, Italianate style station building dates from 1848 and consists of two tall pavilions at either end of a sloping awning, supported by four square columns. Pleasing details include pairs of moulded wooden brackets supporting the roof eaves. On the southbound platform side, the awning is on slender iron columns. Complementing the scene are a cast-iron latticed footbridge, a level crossing and an 1899 Midland Railway signal box (like the station, Grade II listed) which was used as the basis for a popular Airfix model railway kit!

Nearby: Rutland's county town can be explored on foot from this, its only operational station. On the way, a plaque on Hudson's Cottage records it was 'probably' birthplace, in 1619, of the smallest man (18 inches) from England's smallest county. Rutland Railway Museum is out of town, at Cottesmore.

The Grainstore Brewery Tap, Station Approach, Oakham, Rutland, LE15 6RE. Tel. 01572 770065. Daily 11am – midnight (Sunday 11pm). www.grainstorebrewery.com

PEMBROKE DOCK, DYFED

Former Pembroke & Tenby Railway (GWR), terminus of the West Wales line from Carmarthen and Swansea.

STATION INN

Set at an extremity of the old GWR, the ticket office and waiting room of this handsome station have been transformed into a popular freehouse and community pub, known for its cask ales. The building, of granite, was built by the P&TR in 1864 and is Grade II listed. Sadly, the single track comes to a premature end at this heavily rationalized station, no longer continuing into the dockyard. Features such as angled chimneys, pointed windows and saw-tooth valancing combine to create a pleasant scene: it has been spared the total destruction of railway heritage often encountered at end-of-track.

I visited one summer's evening with my family and a friend, a priest who speaks his mind on matters of epicure. We were, at first, the only customers but soon joined by many more, then a

The Station Inn at dusk on a summer evening in 2006.

six-piece jazz band arrived and struck up a number (live music is a regular feature). Two of the three hand-pumps were in use, serving Holdens HB and Young's Bitter. In the Pullman Restaurant – separated from the one-room bar by folding glass doors – we enjoyed a three-course meal from a varied menu (meals available lunchtimes and evenings). When our friend remarked, with a contented smile, 'this is most agreeable,' we knew the pub had passed muster.

The interior, with bare floorboards, church pew seats and bars at the windows, is furnished simply but a sprinkling of railway prints and memorabilia enhances its charm. This ranges from an assortment of brake lamps to a fictional station nameboard – 'Fal Vale', which the landlord rescued from an amateur drama group production of *The Ghost Train.* It transpired that we were drinking with a former CAMRA branch chairman and deputy town mayor: proof, if any were needed, of the pub's community credentials. Winner of awards from the local CAMRA branch, there are seasonal beer festivals. Outdoor seating in summer.

The Station Inn, Hawkestone Road, Pembroke Dock, Dyfed, SA72 6JL. Tel. 01646 621255. Tuesday to Saturday 11am – 2.30pm, 6.30 – 11.30pm (closed Monday), Sunday noon – 2.30pm, 7 – 10.30pm.

PITSFORD & BRAMPTON, NORTHAMPTONSHIRE

Former London & North Western Railway between Northampton and Market Harborough (closed). Partially reopened as Northampton & Lamport Railway (a heritage line).

THE BRAMPTON HALT

A Midland Railway lamp adorns the garden of The Brampton Halt, an extended former stationmaster's house.

This popular pub-restaurant is set around a greatly extended former stationmaster's house in a beauty-spot. Adjacent is a branch line that closed in 1981, now the headquarters of a developing heritage railway. Four real ales are regularly available (Sharp's Doom Bar, Fuller's London Pride, Morland Old Speckled Hen and Adnams Bitter when I called) and the menu is extensive (served all day until 9.30pm, Sunday 9pm), including a barbeque in summer and afternoon teas.

The former branch line corridor has been re-christened the Brampton Valley Way and is a linear country park used by National Cycle Network Route 6. I found cycling from Northampton Station a pleasant way to reach the pub, including views of the West Coast main line. After three miles of mainly level pedalling I glimpsed a semaphore signal and signal box marking the southern extremity of the preserved line. A volunteer engineering gang was re-stringing the telegraph wires.

The old stationmaster's house, which is the pub's nucleus, is the only original railway building surviving at this location, dating from around the time of the line's 1859 opening. In red brick with horizontal courses of yellow, and three upper windows set within pointed arches – their crowns with delicate finials – are indications that this was home to a railway employee of some rank. He would have taken personal charge of any important or urgent shipments arriving or leaving by train, supervised a staff of at least half-a-dozen and come out to meet the main passenger trains. Today, the original entrance has been sealed and a modern glazed canopy placed in front, for smokers' use, detracting from the look somewhat. Nothing original remains inside, though the pub's spacious interior is decorated with railway prints and photographs. Two snugs have been laid out to resemble passenger train compartments, complete with luggage racks! A spacious garden, laid to patio and lawn, with lots of tables and seating, overlooks a small lake and wooded valley. A perfect location for an *al fresco* repast, especially on summer weekends when the sound of a steam locomotive often fills the air. The car park is entered through an old level crossing gate. Beer festival in September. Children welcome.

Nearby: The Northampton & Lamport Railway is maintained by volunteers who run steam or heritage diesel-hauled trains every Sunday from March until October. An array of working semaphores and several signal boxes enhance the attraction. The cycle track/footpath follows its length. Northampton has a restored Art Nouveau house, 78 Derngate, designed in 1917 by Charles Rennie Mackintosh for model railway manufacturer W.J. Bassett-Lowke and displaying some of his models.

The Brampton Halt, Pitsford Road, Chapel Brampton, Northampton, NN6 8BA. Tel. 01604 842676.
Weekdays 11am – midnight (Friday and Saturday 1am), Sunday noon – midnight. Nearest station: Northampton, 3.7 miles, then taxi or cycle. www.thebramptonhalt.co.uk

PORTHMADOG, GWYNEDD (1)

Former Cambrian Railways (GWR) between Barmouth and Pwllheli.

STATION INN

The Cambrian Coast line is one of Britain's most scenic and this is the only licensed station refreshment room on the route from Machynlleth to Pwllheli. Situated in the building on the canopied southbound platform, it is a free house popular with the local community as well as passengers. Its two hand-pumps often dispense one ale from the town's Purple Moose brewery and another from a farther-flung independent, such as Cornwall's Wooden Hand, or Brains from Cardiff. There is a small public bar devoted mainly to sports memorabilia (no hand-pumps) and a larger lounge, which is rather functional but whose walls are decorated with railway photographs, prints and signs, many GWR related. A list shows the prices of refreshments on the Cambrian Railways: very different to today's. A collection of crests above the wood-panelled bar relate not to railways but to Army battalions, Royal Navy ships and the police. There is a pool table and juke-box. Snacks such as sandwiches are served here and in the adjacent café. Outdoor seating in a small garden.

The 'Cambrian Coast Express' at Porthmadog on August 25, 2005, headed by BR 4MT 2-6-0 No. 76079. The Station Inn occupies the single remaining building on the right.

Porthmadog is a passing place on the single track Cambrian Coast route which follows the coast of Cardigan Bay, whose highlight is the Mawddach Estuary crossing at Barmouth on a half-mile long trestle bridge. Before reaching the station, Pwllheli bound trains cross the Welsh Highland Railway on the level. This combined standard and narrow gauge crossing is unique in Britain. Also, the Welsh Highland (Heritage) Railway is across the road from Porthmadog Station.

> **Station Inn, Porthmadog Station, Gwynedd LL49 9HT. Tel. 01766 512629. Daily 11am (Sunday noon) – 11pm (Friday and Saturday midnight).**

PORTHMADOG HARBOUR, GWYNEDD (2)

Terminus of the Ffestiniog Railway to Blaenau Ffestiniog and Welsh Highland Railway to Caernarfon (narrow gauge heritage lines).

SPOONER'S CAFÉ AND BAR

The Ffestiniog Railway is the cradle of narrow gauge, steam-powered railways, dating from 1832 and offering a spectacularly scenic ride behind historic locomotives through the mountains of Snowdonia. Spooner's, meanwhile, has an enviable reputation in the area for its wide range of real ale. That both these superlatives are found side-by-side is one of the wonders of Wales.

The slate-built hostelry started life in the 1880s as the harbourside goods shed. Those sitting outside get a ringside view of the steam trains including, since 2011, those of the re-born Welsh Highland Railway. As befitting an establishment named in honour of the Spooner family (James Spooner was the Ffestiniog's surveyor and builder, while his sons and other family members helped run and manage it for half a century), the interior is filled with railway artefacts. In fact, the 'shed' was a

Princess, an 0-4-0 tank built in 1863, is the largest exhibit in Spooner's, which occupies the old goods shed at Porthmadog Harbour.

museum at one stage and the walls are covered with antique signs and equipment, mostly belonging to this line. Pride of place goes to a full-size locomotive, the railway's No.1, *Princess,* an 0-4-0 tank built in 1863 and far superior to the decorative features in most pubs! (NB: Temporarily removed in late 2012.) There is also a collection of narrow-gauge locomotive nameplates – including the aptly-named *Little Giant* and *Welsh Pony* – a Ffestiniog slotted-post semaphore signal and a 3¼-inch (one-seventh scale) working model, built in 1869, of *Topsy,* a George England 0-4-0 locomotive. The model was once used by Charles Spooner to entertain visitors to his house.

The long bar counter has six hand-pumps with a changing ale selection, mostly from small independent breweries such as Felinfoel, Wye Valley and Porthmadog's own Purple Moose. That company's Snowdonia Ale was first brewed for the Welsh Highland Railway's 2006 Rail Ale Festival and is now a regular feature, having won numerous awards.

Seating includes 'snugs' along one wall and stools at the bar. Meals (including breakfast) can be ordered in the adjoining café for serving in the bar area. Hot meals are available most of the day except for two hours in the afternoon (may be reduced in winter). The popularity of this venue, which has won several awards from the local branch of CAMRA, is such that it will often be standing room only on some summer evenings, with conversations in Welsh and English to be heard. About ten minutes' walk from the National Rail station (see above): via Stryd Fawr (High Street).

Spooner's Café and Bar, Harbour Station, Porthmadog, Gwynedd, LL49 9NF. Tel. 01766 516032. Monday to Saturday 9.30am – 11pm, Sunday noon – 10.30pm. www.festrail.co.uk

RAVENGLASS, CUMBRIA

Former Whitehaven & Furness Junction Railway between Barrow-in-Furness and Whitehaven. (Ravenglass & Eskdale Railway terminus adjacent).

THE RATTY ARMS

The narrow gauge Ravenglass & Eskdale Railway, known colloquially as 'La'al Ratty', has lent its name to this converted station building, full of railway interest, on the northbound main line platform. Built in local stone by the Furness Railway in 1873, a distinctive feature is the integral platform awning. This has been enclosed and glazed to create a galley-shaped dining room and separate passenger waiting shelter. One of the station's old oil lamps has pride of place over the fireplace, with its solid fuel stove for cooler days, and some model railway equipment is on display. There are photographs of the station in steam days and a set of vintage railway prints by C. Hamilton Ellis and a photograph of the Ravenglass & Eskdale when it was a three-foot gauge iron-ore carrier. Lovers of whimsy should read the *Guard's Lament,* penned by a thirsty railwayman following the pub's opening. The building suffered a fire in late 2009, though this did not affect the public areas and the building has been repaired.

Real ales were Theakston Best, Yates Solway Summer and Ruddles Bitter, though Jennings Cumberland Ale is normally also available. Food is served lunchtime and evenings and a flower-decked rear patio provides outdoor seating. Quiz nights, dartboard, dominoes; children are welcome.

Nearby: Opposite, in matching random stone, is the former goods shed, now used for narrow-gauge loco maintenance and, near the footbridge, is the Furness Railway signal box, a tall, stone structure with weatherboarding. In the former good yard is a narrow gauge railway museum. The Ravenglass & Eskdale Railway started life as a three-foot gauge industrial line in 1875 but was revived as a 15-inch miniature route by model-maker W.J. Bassett-Lowke in 1916. A chequered history followed but, since its most recent revival in 1961, it has been a popular heritage railway. The steam engines take passengers on a seven-mile ride into the Lake District National Park. One of them, *River Irt,* is the world's oldest working 15-inch gauge locomotive, built in 1894.

The Ratty Arms, Ravenglass, Cumbria, CA18 1SN. Tel. 01229 717676. Monday to Saturday 11am – 11pm, Sunday noon – 10.30pm. From October to Easter, closes 3 – 5.30pm weekdays.

The Ratty Arms, with diesel unit 156 475 departing northwards in May 2010.

Above left: A new use for Reading's Italianate GWR station building Above right: *'Hymek' Class 35 7028 enters Reading with a train for Worcester on March 4, 1972: well before The Three Guineas, now off the right-hand side, opened.*

READING, BERKSHIRE

Former Great Western Railway main line between London Paddington and Bristol and other routes.

THE THREE GUINEAS

This is surely the only station to carry a plaque in memory of someone killed by a whirlwind. Twenty-four year-old carpenter Henry West was whisked off an earlier station roof in 1840. Another sign, this time outside the pub, asserts: 'Over 500 real ales will be served in the next 12 months.' The 'Guineas' occupies much of the Grade II listed, Italianate station building constructed by the GWR in 1870, neatly topped with its square cupola and clock. Railway business and other retail functions are now carried out in a modern structure next door, opened by the Queen in 1989.

The single, split-level bar, with upholstered bench seating and sofas, is cavernous. There is a railway themed corner including postcards, prints and historical photos – though none of the old Reading West signal box, one of the GWR's largest boxes. The town was home to the Great Western Signal Works, producing most of the equipment used on its network until closure in 1984. Other decoration is sports oriented, including the five television screens and the pub is busy when London Irish or Reading FC are playing at Madejski Stadium. 'The Three Guineas' refers to a prize awarded to joint winners of a 1904 competition to name a crack GWR train running 245 miles non-stop from London to Plymouth. The winning name was 'The Riviera Express'.

A honeypot for ale lovers, on my visit, all eight hand-pumps were in use, six dispensing beer from small regional or micro-breweries such as Nethergate, Cairngorm and Springhead. Despite a minor heatwave, the beer was cool and in good condition. It was enjoyable to be able to see the trains, including HSTs, arrive and depart on platform four. The station is undergoing a major £850 million redevelopment and expansion, with completion in 2015, to cope with an expected doubling of passengers to 28 million a year.

A wide menu is served all day every day, including Sunday roast dinners. There's train arrival and departure information; background music, and live music some evenings. Outside dining area to front. Access is from the street only, none from the platform.

The Three Guineas, Station Approach, Reading, Berkshire, RG1 1LY. Tel. 0118 957 2743. Monday to Saturday 10am – 11pm, Sunday noon – 10.30pm. www.three-guineas.co.uk

RIBBLEHEAD, NORTH YORKSHIRE

Former Midland Railway between
Settle and Appleby.

THE STATION INN

A place of shelter, real ale, good food and hospitality on one of the greatest and most remote lines in England. If buildings could speak, what tales this place could tell, in such a bleak setting, with only the railway and fells for company. The Settle & Carlisle Railway needs little introduction: the last of the great main lines, built the old fashioned way in the 1870s by pick, shovel and the brawn of an army of navvies. They created a superbly engineered line, linking England with Scotland for the Midland Railway, with many great tunnels and viaducts, across one of the wildest, most inhospitable parts of the country. Its largest structure, and *cause célèbre* when the line was under threat of closure, is Ribblehead Viaduct, one hundred feet high and 24 arches long.

Built about the same time as the railway, this inn looks out to the viaduct and Batty Moss, now barren but once bustling with a brick works and a large shanty town, Batty Green. Its one hundred wooden huts housed two thousand navvies and their families. They lived for years in crowded, insanitary conditions. (Other shanty settlements were given names such as Sebastopol, Jericho and Jerusalem.) Despite the best efforts of visiting missionaries, the navvies were hard drinking men who frequently ran amok in the inns and villages and angered locals. Much of the drinking stayed within the shanties, but there is a tale of an inebriated navvy throwing dynamite on the fire at the nearby Gearstones Inn, injuring customers and blowing a kettle to pieces. Another is reputed to have sold his wife for a barrel of beer. Picture scenes from the Wild West and you'll not be far wrong.

The weather here is as wild as the landscape and the inn is faced with corrugated iron on its south-west wall to give extra protection from the elements. Someone has a sense of humour as there is a 'weather forecasting stone' near the entrance bearing the witty notice: 'Swinging stone = windy; Stone gone = tornado.'

Of the two public rooms, one is carpeted and set out for diners, with local railway prints and photos, the other with a public bar feel including a woodblock floor, juke-box, pool table and simple slate fireplace with wood-burning stove and decorated with cast-iron wagon plates. There is a model of a four-wheeled van, grandly named the 'Contractor's Hotel'. The real thing provided portable living quarters for up to ten engineers and its arrival on Batty Moss in autumn 1869 signalled the start of the preliminary work on the viaduct. Those less lucky had to camp in tents and their supplies were delivered by donkey. Another pub feature is the 'Loo with a View': the gent's toilet looks out on to the viaduct! A previous customer was Michael Portillo while filming his *Great British Railway Journeys* for the BBC. As Minister of State for Transport under Margaret Thatcher, he reprieved the line from threat of closure. The landlord told me he was sure that, had the railway closed, the inn would have shut for good.

There are six hand-pumps on a semi-circular, stone-built bar, with beers sourced from the region. A local Dent Brewery ale and Black Sheep Bitter are regulars, and the two guests on my visit were from Skipton's Copper Dragon Brewery. A menu, using local meat, cheese and other produce, is served daily, lunchtime and evening, with hours extended at weekends and on school holidays. Bed and breakfast and bunkhouse accommodation is available.

Nearby: The station, a restored Midland Railway structure typical of the line, houses a small visitors' centre open daily in summer. Walkers can follow the Dales Way past the viaduct towards the entrance of 2,629 yard Blea Moor Tunnel. The next station north, Dent, is the highest in England on a main line, at 1,150 feet.

The Station Inn, Ribblehead, near Ingleton,
North Yorkshire, LA6 3AS. Tel. 01524 241274.
150 yards from station on B6255. Daily 11am – 11pm.
www.thestationinn.net

A Class 47 accelerates past The Station Inn with a train from Carlisle, after crossing Ribblehead Viaduct, on 31 August, 1982.

RUSHDEN, NORTHAMPTONSHIRE

Former Midland Railway branch from
Wellingborough to Higham Ferrers (closed).
Part reopened as a heritage railway and museum.

RUSHDEN HISTORICAL TRANSPORT
SOCIETY SOCIAL CLUB

Every evening at dusk a volunteer carefully lights the gas lamps dotted around the former ladies' waiting room housing this atmospheric bar. Their warm glow brightens the room, and a gentle hiss from the gas jets accompanies the buzz of conversation. On the platform the doors of a former British Railways' parcels carriage are swung open to reveal the bar lounge, set with armchairs and sofa at one end and a skittles table at the other. There are occasional tables and a fully stocked bookcase; while vintage brewery posters and train photos decorate the walls. 'On events days the mobile lounge steams off to end of track for a while, but if you're on board with your pint, be patient and you'll be back here in no time,' says a helpful club member. Alternatively, sit on a platform bench with your drink, soaking up the period branch line atmosphere. There are flower baskets and porters' trolleys, and enamel signs advertising delights such as Palethorpe's sausages, Senior Service cigarettes and Harry Sell's 'Game, Fish & Poultry'.

The bar's seven hand-pumps are busy. With a turnover of around 20 barrels weekly, the beers change frequently. A board displays which are 'on' and which are nearly ready. A former porters' room beneath serves as the cellar, with a stick beaten on the ceiling apparently used to communicate between the bar and cellar personnel! The selection on my visit included Phipps Northampton Brewery IPA (something of a legend in these parts, the defunct brewery's ale is being brewed again by Grainstore in Oakham using the 1930s recipe, its hoppy flavour suited to the palates of local shoe workers); RCH IPA, two from Nuneaton brewery Church End (Goat's Milk and Stout Coffin), Oakham Bishop's Farewell and Salopian Golden Thread. There is always a

A cosy corner of the bar at Rushden (note gas lamps).

dark beer and real cider available. The venue has twice been declared National Club of the Year by CAMRA.

The walls are filled with period enamel advertisements and train photos, while a collection of beer trays and bottles is arranged neatly around the room. Level crossing 'gates', complete with lamp, divide the split-level bar; there is a piano, used for honky-tonk evenings, and a coal fire completing the scene. A book kept behind the bar depicts a 1950s' circus elephant, with its glamorous trainer, in the goods yard, having arrived here by train! Though a members' bar, visitors are always welcome.

Rushden Station was once derelict and overgrown, and came close to demolition to accommodate a new road scheme. The Society (first convened in a local pub in 1976) campaigned hard, purchasing the lease in 1996 and working tirelessly on restoration ever since. In June 2009, passenger carrying trains ran again on a short stretch of track, 50 years to the day after the last scheduled service on the branch. Passenger traffic ceased in 1959, with goods and parcels lasting a further ten years. The bar, opened in 1985, provides a source of funds for the restoration work. Built of red brick by the Midland Railway and opened in 1894, the station building, on a sloping site, has two storeys, with its platform at the upper level. Aside from the bar, there's a transport museum and restored stationmaster's office and booking hall. A Midland signal box is a preservation era addition. No food is served, though snacks include pickled eggs and pork scratchings. Children and dogs welcome. Beer takeaways available. Annual beer festival.

Rushden Transport Museum, Station Approach, Rushden, Northamptonshire, NN10 0AW. Tel. 01933 318988. Monday to Friday 7.30 – 11pm, Saturday noon – 11pm, Sunday noon – 10.30pm. Non-members pay £1 for day membership (free on events days). Museum opens weekends, Easter to October (admission free). Nearest station: Wellingborough (five miles). www.rhts.co.uk

SHEFFIELD, SOUTH YORKSHIRE

Former Midland Railway main line from
London St. Pancras and other routes.

THE SHEFFIELD TAP

Reopened after a long period of neglect in 2009, this is a breathtaking revival of the First Class Railway Refreshment Room of 1904, part of Grade II listed Sheffield Midland. Period features such as a terrazzo floor and full-length Minton wall tiling have been restored, while a coved ceiling with its sky-lights has been replaced, the original having partially collapsed. Thanks to large arched windows fronting the platform, the room is filled with natural light. It is hard to believe that this was a run-down waiting room in the 1970s and reduced to storeroom status by the late eighties. The restoration, a labour of love for local businessmen Jamie Hawksworth and Jon Holdsworth, was grant-aided by the Railway Heritage Trust and received a National Railway Heritage Award in 2010.

The Sheffield Tap.

A mahogany bar counter and the original, ornately carved bar back, set with mirrors and a central clock, runs almost the full length of the wall; there is a replica period fireplace and a snug, leading to the street exit, once a taxi office. In late 2010 the bar was extended into a hallway where second class customers were once served, creating a second snug. The team's next project is to expand into an adjacent former dining room, restoring its grandeur and installing a micro-brewery. The absence of kitchens precludes reinstatement of a meal service.

Attention to architectural detail is matched by a choice of drinks which usually includes at least four ales from Thornbridge Brewery in Derbyshire (a partner in this project), plus four guest ales and a range of continental beers served from 12 swing-handled taps, including Bernard Pilsner from the Czech Republic and Sierra Nevada from the USA. There is further choice from a selection of some 200 bottled beers from Europe, the USA and beyond. There is outdoor seating on the street side and level access from both platform and street. Cold snacks include paninis and cakes, accompanied by pots of Yorkshire tea as well as coffee. Ambient music, dogs welcome.

The station and nearby: With its 1904 expansion, Sheffield Midland became the largest on the Midland Railway after St Pancras. Its renovation in recent years has included glazing of the large *porte-cochère* which now forms part of a spacious expanded concourse. This leads to a piazza complete with water feature. Ornamentation around the station includes stone arches engraved with MR monograms and emblems, swirly iron fan grilles, glazed awnings and decorative chimney-pots. The city offers rich pickings for pub and ale lovers, while the street-running Supertram lends something of a continental air. About five minutes' walk from the station is the Rutland Arms (junction of Brown and Furnival Streets), serving local ales and meals, its features including engraved and stained glass panels. The Kelham Island district has two excellent pubs, the Kelham Island Tavern (CAMRA's national pub of the year two years running) and the Fat Cat.

The Sheffield Tap, Platform 1B, Sheffield Station, Sheaf Street, Sheffield S1 2BP. Tel. 0114 273 7558. Sunday to Thursday 11am – 11pm, Friday and Saturday 10am – midnight. www.sheffieldtap.com

SOWERBY BRIDGE, WEST YORKSHIRE

Former Lancashire & Yorkshire Railway, between Halifax/Brighouse and Manchester (Victoria).

JUBILEE REFRESHMENT ROOMS

Two railway enthusiast brothers have achieved something that would be a dream job for many: serving real ale in their own lovingly restored station building. Chris and Andrew Wright spent ten years negotiating with officialdom and returning the structure, a former ticket office dating from 1876 but disused for a quarter-century, to life. They achieved this and opened in 2009 with the help of the Railway Heritage Trust. 'Jubilee' was added to the title in honour of a locomotive class that once gave sterling

The Jubilee Refreshment Rooms.

service on the line. Interior walls have been removed to create a long, bright room. Furnishing and decoration is contemporary and restrained. At one end is a brick chimney breast with a solid fuel stove; at the other, a stylish wooden bar with six hand-pumps serves a changing selection of Lancashire and Yorkshire ales. On my visit these were from Millstone, Old Spot, Ilkley, Old Mill, Elland and Saltaire. There is a range of bottled European beers and lagers, and cider. Sandwiches, cakes and light refreshments are served. Breakfasts are served until noon, except Sunday.

There are local railway prints and photographs, vintage enamel brewery signs and a distinctive clock from a Halifax jeweller's shop. One set (of four) hand-pumps once graced The Tandem pub in Waterloo, Huddersfield. A large print shows the full extent of Sowerby Bridge station buildings before a fire swept through them in the 1970s, leading to the greater part being demolished. Today's refreshment room, adjacent to the Manchester-bound platform, formed one wing of the building but is all that remains. It served as both a booking office, until 1983, and a lamp room and mess room for permanent way staff until 1997. There are occasional exhibitions of railway or brewery interest. CAMRA Calderdale pub of the year, 2012.

This was not the first station on the site. An earlier structure was notable as a place of work, briefly, for the Brontë sisters'

This Edwardian postcard shows the extent of Sowerby Bridge Station before a fire in the 1970s. Today's refreshment rooms occupy the surviving single-storey block on the left.

wayward brother Branwell (their parsonage home at Haworth is 13 miles distant). Sowerby Bridge was once an important junction on the L&Y main line, though only traces remain of the extensive acreage the railway covered. A locomotive shed closed in 1964; the current station dates from the 1980s.

Nearby: Trains from Halifax approach Sowerby Bridge via the Copley Viaduct of 1852, which crosses the Calder Valley on 21 arches. It is one of the railway wonders of Yorkshire. The Wainhouse Tower can be seen from trains crossing it. This Victorian folly was designed by eccentric industrialist John Edward Wainhouse as a chimney to be linked underground to a nearby factory. Never used as such, it has been restored and is occasionally open to the public, providing spectacular views for those who climb to the top.

> **The Jubilee Refreshment Rooms, Station Road, Sowerby Bridge, West Yorkshire, HX6 3AB. Tel. 01422 648285. Monday to Friday 9.30am – 10pm, Saturday 9am – 10pm (licensed from noon), Sunday noon – 10pm. www.jubileerefreshmentrooms.co.uk**

STALYBRIDGE, GREATER MANCHESTER

Former London & North Western Railway between Manchester and Huddersfield.

STATION BUFFET BAR

A large clock at the Manchester end of platform one marks the entrance to a bar that has achieved iconic status among ale lovers and railway enthusiasts. They come from far and wide, many following the Trans-Pennine Real Ale Trail. The structure dates from a station rebuild in 1885 and the interior boasts a place on CAMRA's Regional Inventory of historic pub interiors. In fact there has been a licensed bar of some kind on the station since at least 1860. There is a record of one Hugh Toney being sentenced to seven days' hard labour in the 1870s for being drunk and disorderly and taking a glass worth sixpence.

The bar's survival is largely thanks to railway enthusiast and publican John Hesketh, who took over the hostelry in January 1997, following a campaign to save it from closure. He filled it with railway ephemera, brought in micro-brewery ales and single-handedly created a legendary destination boozer. He died in October 2011 and it is now leased to Mike Field and Sarah Barnes of the West Riding Refreshment Rooms, Dewsbury (q.v.). There are two compact rooms, one containing a marble-topped bar counter; the other was the first class ladies' waiting room. Both are filled with a variety of railway artefacts that would do justice to a small museum. An adjoining horseshoe-shaped conservatory was rebuilt in 2009, complete with etched glass windows. Lord Pendry of Stalybridge is among the regulars and contributed towards a refurbishment of the back room in 2012. The station clock outside is a replica: the original is in the National Railway Museum, York.

Eight hand-pumps provide a variety of ales, mainly from micro-breweries and including Titanic First Class, Boddingtons, Timothy Taylor Landlord, Millstone Three B's and two from Greenfield – Black Five and Winter Hop – on my last visit. There was also farm cider and some foreign bottled beers. A board

The Station Buffet Bar pictured in 2003.

proudly declared '7,785 guest ales since January 1997'.

The mixture of locals firmly-rooted to the spot and passengers of all ages 'just passing through' gives the place a certain energy and a visit at any time of day is worthwhile. I once called in for a delicious cooked breakfast – complete with black pudding – early on a January morning, when there were already several other customers, and spoke with a man lighting the fire by deftly holding sheets of newspaper against the stone fireplace to create a draught. At other times the place is buzzing with the sound of conversation (there are no games machines or juke-box) the only other distractions being the occasional train trundling in. There is a thriving Station Railway Society which meets once a month to discuss matters connected with railways and transport.

A range of hot and cold snacks and meals, often including sausage and mash, liver and onions and a roast of the day, is served daily until 6.30pm. Also paninis and burgers, plus 'famous black peas', a local delicacy. On the counter top a glass cabinet, jostling for space with vintage Oxo tins, uniform caps and three flat-irons, includes souvenirs for sale. Outdoor seating. Children allowed until early evening; dogs welcome.

On the station: A plaque on platform one is devoted to railwayman and hero Fred Wood who, in 1907, prevented many deaths when he switched the points to divert a runaway heavy goods train, avoiding a collision with a busy workers' train. Overlooked by the Pennines, the station is terminus of the once-weekly 'parliamentary' service which runs, in one direction only, from Stockport via Reddish South and Denton on Friday mornings. It is apparently cheaper to run this than go through the process of closing the line.

Station Buffet Bar, Platform One, Stalybridge Station, Rassbottom Street, Stalybridge, Greater Manchester, SK15 1RF. Tel. 0161 303 0007. Weekdays 10am – 11pm (licensed from 11am), Sunday noon – 10.30pm. www.buffetbar.org

The Buffet Bar and replica station clock at Stalybridge in 2005.

STOCKPORT, GREATER MANCHESTER

Former London & North Western Railway, on West Coast main line between Manchester Piccadilly and Wilmslow, Macclesfield and other destinations.

THE CROWN INN

Though not occupying a railway structure, this award-winning pub is dramatically sited beneath one of the country's greatest viaducts, which towers over it like a striding giant. Popular with ale enthusiasts for its wide range of micro-brewery beers, the Crown retains the atmosphere and some features of a Victorian multi-room pub. There are four rooms leading from a compact bar, including a rear snug, a lounge with feature overmantel and cosy front parlour retaining its bell-pushes from which customers would have summoned table service. The runner-up for CAMRA's National Pub of the Year in 2008, it serves 16 frequently changing ales, often including Copper Dragon, Pictish and Phoenix, with real cider too.

At the time of its construction in 1841 by the Manchester & Birmingham Railway, Stockport's viaduct was the world's largest built of brick. Six hundred men toiled on its 27 arches, 22 of which span 63ft at heights up to 111ft. It crosses the valley of the Mersey, already a built-up area when work started, including cottages from which the pub was converted. It was widened in 1887 and depicted in works by 'matchstick men' painter L.S. Lowry. Newspaper cuttings describing the building project decorate the pub's hallway, while a cobbled yard to the rear (also used for live music sessions) allows customers to drink in the shadow of the behemoth. Bar meals are served at lunchtime Monday to Friday.

Nearby: There is a wide choice of other real ale pubs and an established Stockport Ale Trail. Historic gems include the Arden Arms and Swan With Two Necks. The Hat Works is a museum dedicated to the local hatting industry; the nineteenth century Market Hall is a riot of glass, iron and steel.

The Crown Inn, 154 Heaton Lane, Stockport SK4 1AR. Tel. 0161 480 5850. On foot: Ten minutes from station (left along Wellington Road, then left after river bridge into Heaton Lane). Daily noon – 11pm (Sunday 10.30pm). www.thecrowninn110mb.com

The Crown Inn, with Stockport's massive viaduct rising above.

SWINDON, WILTSHIRE

Former Great Western Railway main line from London (Paddington) to Bristol (Temple Meads) and other destinations.

THE GLUE POT

Little remains of the ornate station refreshment rooms where, for 54 years, every GWR train was required to stop so first and second class passengers could take sustenance before continuing their journey (see page 12). However, to sample a hostelry that generations of GWR workers would have known, one just has to walk nine minutes' east of the station into Brunel's Railway

Village, dating from 1843. At the end of one of the handsome terraces the company provided for the fitters and toolmakers of Swindon Works, stands this Grade II listed corner pub. Built in limestone for the GWR during the same decade, it is a simple, one-room pub with no frills or fancy decoration. The prime attraction is an ever-changing selection of eight real ales and five ciders. As a tied house of the Hop Back Brewery, one will always find several ales from this Salisbury brewer and its neighbour Downton; as well as White Horse, named after the Vale through which the railway runs, and, to quote the barman, a 'surprise' or two. Blackboards keep customers up-to-date with brews available and being prepared.

Though not the oldest of the trio of Railway Village pubs – that distinction goes to the Cricketers (1847), popular with the GWR cricket team, on the other side of Emlyn Square – the Glue Pot, previously a shop, was licensed in the early 1850s. Around 1900 it was called the London Stout Tavern but later gained its current title in deference to the coachbuilders for whom it became the drinking hole of choice (loco men socialised separately from carriage workers). It was also known unofficially as Charlie Thomas's, after a 1940s landlord, later gaining a reputation as a scrumpy house. Dorothy Grimes, one-time bar lady whose father was a GWR labourer, recalled:

'In the wartime blackout Charlie would strike a match, check the till and if he thought he had taken enough over the bar would shut up early. There was sawdust on the floor and spittoons...a coke 'tortoise heater' stood in the middle...with a big pipe coming out the back.'

Seating provision today is mainly high-backed wooden settles, arranged with their heavy wooden tables around distinctive windows. There is no sign of the above-mentioned stove, but the pub retains its separate entrance, corridor and serving hatch for off-sales – a once common feature, now seen rarely. There are no distractions such as a juke-box or games machines, though on my visit jazz and blues music was playing. Meals are served Wednesday to Friday lunchtimes; dogs are welcome; roadside patio.

Nearby: Steam Museum, housed in part of the former railway works, tells the story of 'God's Wonderful Railway.'

The Glue Pot, 5 Emlyn Square, Swindon, Wiltshire, SN1 5BP. Tel. 01793 325993. Monday 4.30 – 11pm, Tuesday to Saturday noon – 11pm (Fri./ Sat. opens 11.30am), Sunday noon – 10.30pm. From station: Right out of station, along Station Road/Sheppard Street/London Street, left into Emlyn Square. www.hopback.co.uk

URMSTON, GREATER MANCHESTER

Former Cheshire Lines Committee, between Warrington (Central) and Manchester (Oxford Road).

THE STEAMHOUSE

This externally pleasing renovation of a station building dating from 1872, occupied by a pub opened in 2008, has won plaudits from CAMRA for the quality and variety of its ales. Its interior decor comes as a surprise, however, being a rather kitsch modern take on a medieval great hall. Train watchers benefit from bench seating on a fenced-off part of the Warrington-bound platform.

The brick building features Gothic-style pointed windows and doorways, slate roofs with deep eaves and decorative chimney-pots; the platform awning has been removed. Up to eight regional ales are served, with examples from Hornbeam, Phoenix, All Gates and Dunham when I visited, and some Belgian bottled beer. Meals, including breakfast, are served all afternoon with a carvery on Sunday (booking advisable).

The Steamhouse, Station Approach, Station Road, Urmston, M41 9SB. Tel. 0161 748 6487. Monday to Saturday 11am – 11pm, Fri/Sat to 1am, Sunday 10am – midnight. www.thesteamhouse.co.uk

The Steamhouse at Urmston, looking towards Warrington.

WAINFLEET, LINCOLNSHIRE

Former Great Northern Railway between Sleaford and Skegness.

THE WINDMILL BAR

A bar in a creeper-clad old windmill may seem a bizarre inclusion in a book of railway pubs. This unusual brewery tap was declared Best Railway Pub by the Association of Community Rail Partnerships (ACoRP) in 2007. Like many breweries, family-run Bateman's, established nearby in 1874, often used its local line to ship and receive produce. Since at least 2005, when the 'Poacher Line' was one of the first Community Railways to be designated by the Department for Transport, the company has given its active support to the passenger service.

Arrival at Wainfleet All Saints from the Boston direction is across the pancake-flat Fenlands. The diesel trains seem to sail across this sparsely populated area with its web of drainage ditches and sluices. Leave the train here and, once the signalman has opened the level crossing gates and lowered the semaphore signal with a 'clang,' all is eerily quiet. The brewery is five minutes' walk. Its windmill tower – minus sails but topped with a beer bottle weather vane – houses the bar, its circular wall lined with family portraits and awards. Above is a shelf with scores of vintage beer bottles. Ales usually include Dark Mild, XB Bitter, the malty, hoppy XXXB and a seasonal special. If you are lucky, the menu will include the complex Salem Porter; bottled Belgian and Czech beers are also available. Food is served in the bar or adjacent bistro from noon until 2pm daily. Sunday lunch is a speciality.

Several times a year one can arrive in style on the Music Train from Sleaford, a scheduled service which, on these occasions, carries musicians and a party atmosphere prevails. Passengers disembark here for a Lincolnshire supper and beer sampling. Tours of the Victorian brewhouse and a new one opened in 2002 run regularly. Visitors can try their hand at traditional pub games now rarely seen, such as shove shive, target bowls and cheese skittles. Beer festival in October.

Bateman's Salem Bridge Brewery, Mill Lane, Wainfleet, Lincolnshire PE24 4JE. Tel. 01754 882009/882017. Wednesday to Sunday 11.30am – 4pm (not January). Closes 2.30pm October to March. Tours Wednesday to Sunday, contact brewery for times. www.bateman.co.uk

Bateman's Brewery, home to the circular Windmill Bar.

WAUNFAWR, GWYNEDD

Welsh Highland Railway (narrow gauge heritage line) between Caernarfon and Porthmadog.

SNOWDONIA PARK

Set in a mountain valley where slopes rise steadily toward Snowdon, this former stationmaster's house is one of the most spectacularly sited brewpubs. Home to the Snowdonia Brewery (see page 134), out of sight in the basement, it also provides grandstand views of the powerful Garratts and other locomotives on this re-born railway, fully reopened in 2011. The lounge is the oldest part of the building, dating from 1880 when the stopping place was part of the North Wales Narrow Gauge Railway, the WHR's predecessor. With two rough-hewn slate walls, one with a fireplace, built to keep out the worst of the winter weather. Doors open to the front garden which has bench seating. The main bar is at the rear, in a modern and rather soul-less large extension, with a slate-built counter. Picture windows provide panoramic views; there is a juke-box, dartboard and family room. Photographs in the corridor include one of the station *circa* 1923. (At one time the WHR had four small station refreshment rooms, a surprising number for such a diminutive line.) The three regular ales are Aur Eryri Gold (4% ABV), Carmen Sutra (4.4) and WHB West Highland Bitter (5.2); there are often guest beers, too. The station is reached via a footbridge from the pub car park. Meals are served daily, from breakfast until 8.30pm. Play equipment in garden; children and dogs welcome; camping facilities.

On-train drinking: Many WHR trains serve draught real ale from a specially designed hand-pull in the kitchen car. Beer is racked into a polypin by the local Purple Moose Brewery.

Snowdonia Park Brewpub, Waunfawr, Caernarfon, Gwynedd, LL55 4AQ. (On A4085.) Tel. 01286 650409. Daily 11am – 11pm (Friday/Saturday 11.30pm). www.snowdonia-park.co.uk

The Snowdonia Park brewpub, with Waunfawr Station below.

WEMYSS BAY, RENFREWSHIRE

Terminus of the former Caledonian Railway
from Paisley and Glasgow.

STATION BAR (NO REAL ALE)

Situated under the steel and glass roof of a remarkable
Edwardian station, this diminutive bar is easily missed by those
rushing for the Isle of Bute ferry waiting alongside. Early
photographs show it was the second class refreshment room,
equipped with little more than tables and chairs; a bar counter
was fitted later. Decorative wood panelling with a *faux* antique
finish, upholstered bench seating, postcard displays depicting
long departed Clyde steamers of the Caledonian Steam Packet
Company and, on cooler days, a fire ablaze in the hearth,
combine to create the ambience of an elegant era. Stools are
lined up neatly along a plain bar counter which is immaculately
kept, along with its mirrored bar-back. Though popular with
visitors in season, this is a locals' bar too; a place for
conversation where the topic will often be the pride they have
in their station. The Friends of Wemyss Bay Station, established
in 2009 and numbering 250, not only maintain the long-
established tradition of floral displays but run a second-hand
bookshop and gallery on the concourse.

Meals are prepared in the former Tea Room, now the Coffee
Cup Café, separated from the bar by a shared kitchen. The café
is as bright as a button, its tables set with flowers and
newspapers neatly displayed. Simple hot meals are served until
2pm, followed by afternoon tea until 4.30pm (with home baked
biscuits and scones). There are two quirky features. The bar only
possesses a ladies' toilet, gentlemen having to walk across the
concourse; and the telephone is apparently out of earshot of
everyone. So if there's no answer, do not assume they are closed!

The station: Often described as Scotland's most beautiful
station, this was a replacement built in 1903 to the designs of
James Miller and Donald Matheson, who also rebuilt Glasgow
Central. The focal point is a semi-circular ticket office on the

Above: *The Station Bar.*
Below: *The distinctive ticket office at Wemyss Bay.*

concourse with slender glazing extending from its roof like a giant fan. The glazing covers the concourse and continues down a wooden covered walkway to the pier, ending at an arch decorated with twin Japanese-style towers. The exterior is equally striking: a long, curving frontage finished in white pebbledash with sandstone footings, *faux* half-timbering, red-tiled roofs and a carriage entrance, dominated by a tall clock-tower that is a landmark from land and sea.

A 1930s' view of West Bay, with a GWR camping coach and mineral wagons occupying sidings long since removed.

Station Bar, Pierhead, Greenock Road, Wemyss Bay, Renfrewshire, PA18 6AA. Tel. 01475 521265.
Monday to Thursday 11am – 11pm,
Friday and Saturday 10am – midnight
(café opens 7.30am), Sunday 12.30 – 11pm.

WEST BAY, DORSET (station closed)

Former terminus of the Bridport Railway
(GWR) from Maiden Newton.

THE TEA STATION (UNLICENSED)

This restored station, now a tea-shop selling filter coffee, cakes and cream teas, is a short stroll from a beach and harbour on the 'Jurassic Coast' of Lyme Bay. A length of track remains, along with cast-iron lamps and a semaphore signal; tables are set out under an iron-bracketed canopy on the platform. The handsome stone building of 1884, designed by William Clarke, was similar to one at Abbotsbury and is unusual in that it can only be entered from the platform. Inside, the former waiting room is painted Wedgwood blue, filled with historical images of the location and dining tables decorated with gingham table-cloths and flowers. An original fireplace remains.

The station opened when the nine-mile branch was extended from Bridport in anticipation of hotel development that never happened. Passenger trains, which once included an early morning one for swimmers, ceased as early as 1930. Goods traffic, mainly wagons of beach gravel, survived until 1962. The building's fortunes have since been mixed. First adapted as a dwelling, it was uncared for, becoming derelict in the eighties before being renovated in the late 1990s as a council office, until its current role. The goods yard where, in the 1930s, holidaymakers could utilize a GWR camping coach, is now a car park but you can walk a length of the track-bed towards Bridport. Children's playground and toilets adjacent.

Nearby: West Bay is well served by pubs and eating places and there are good cliff walks. In Bridport, Palmers Brewery, with its waterwheel, is the country's oldest thatched brewery and there is a daily tour.

The Tea Station, West Bay Road, Bridport,
Dorset, DT6 4EL. Daily April to October
10.30am – 5pm (subject to weather conditions)
Nearest stations: Dorchester, Maiden Newton.

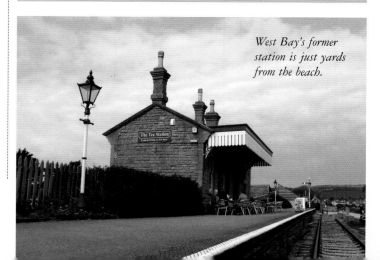

West Bay's former station is just yards from the beach.

WESTON-SUPER-MARE, SOMERSET

*Former Great Western Railway main line
between Bristol Temple Meads and Taunton.*

OFF THE RAILS

Ensconced in a stone-built station of 1884, this compact hostelry is half bar and half buffet. During my visit, on a Saturday afternoon, the bar became busy with locals of both sexes yet the buffet, its tables clad in flowery plastic cloths, was deserted. It reminded me of student parties where everyone congregates around the supply of drink. The contrast was exaggerated by the fact that two televisions, one at each end of the bar section, were broadcasting competing sporting events – a Tottenham v. Blackburn football match and Ireland v. Wales Six Nations rugby. Each had a set of customers following one game or the other, plus there was general banter going on, making it all rather frenetic but good-humoured.

Competitively priced ale, sourced from West Country micro-breweries, is a key attraction, with one from railway oriented brewer RCH's stable (see page 132) a permanent fixture. The two guests were Bath Ales' Dark Hare and Cheddar Ales' Pot Holer. Farmhouse Cider is also available. A white board details those current and coming up. All are kept in condition with the help of a special cooling system in the cellar. Food, served in the buffet area, is snack fare such as sandwiches, pies and pasties. Juke-box; dogs are welcome in bar; no alcohol or glasses outside on platform. Access is from both the platform and the road. Carry-out ale available.

The station: With its integral footbridge and glazed ironwork canopies (restored and rationalized in 1992) this is set on a gentle curve. There are traditional GWR benches and potted palms lend a continental air. On the road side, the long, single storey frontage retains its lengthy awning and the eaves are topped by four decorative finials. Regular steam haulage returns on summer Sundays in the form of the 'Torbay Express' from Bristol to Kingswear. A stone signal box of 1866, a relic of a former station, stands near the approach road at the station's Bristol end.

Off The Rails, Platform Two, Station Approach,
Weston-super-Mare, Somerset, BS23 1XY.
Tel. (01934) 415109.
Daily 7am – 11pm (Sunday 8am).

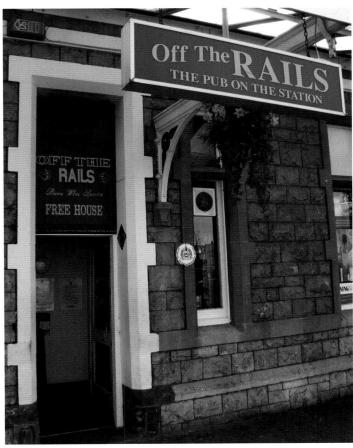

There are entrances to Off the Rails from both platform and pavement: this is the latter.

WINDSOR & ETON CENTRAL, BERKSHIRE

Terminus of former Great Western
Railway branch from Slough.

ALL BAR ONE

There can't be many bars where you can sip a beer or coffee while sitting next to Queen Victoria's water closet. This establishment incorporates the royal waiting room built for the queen whose early patronage made rail travel so popular. Outside the bar, near the single platform from which the diesel units now depart, stands a full-size replica of the 4-2-2 GWR Achilles class locomotive, *The Queen,* the original of which once pulled the royal train.

Built of Bath stone, the waiting room carries two sets of carved crowns and ciphers on each side: one Victoria's, dated 1897 and the other Edward VII's, added in 1902 for his Coronation when a room for gentlemen was also provided. Customers can still see the saloon, Victoria's private retiring room complete with its hand basin and adjacent lavatory.

Windsor's former royal waiting room in 2007, when it was the Ha Ha Bar.

Left: *A full-size replica of Dean Single 4-2-2 No. 3041* The Queen, *built for Madame Tussauds, is an exhibit at Windsor & Eton Central.*

The waiting room proper has carved oak doors, a fireplace and ceiling complete with ornate, Art Nouveau glass dome. Last use of the rooms by royalty was George VI in 1936.

Sharp's Doom Bar was the one real ale on my visit. Food is an important part of the offer here and a wide menu is served all day. There is a spacious outdoor seating area, set beneath the glazed train-shed, built at Victoria's request to 'keep her soldiers dry'.

The station: Replacing a simple Brunel-style wooden train-shed, the rebuilt Central opened in 1897 to mark Victoria's Diamond Jubilee. It is one of the Thames-side town's two rail termini; both are Grade II listed. (The other is Riverside, end of the former London & South Western's branch from Staines, a Gothic building also with former royal waiting rooms, both stations being a short canter from Windsor Castle.) The vast area, most of it under a canopy of iron and glass, beneath which soldiers would form escorts to and from the trains on ceremonial occasions, is now almost completely dedicated to shopping and dining. It has been renamed Windsor Royal Shopping. In the 1980s it was used by Madame Tussaud's for the Royalty and Railways exhibition, recreating the pomp of Victoria's jubilee. The replica locomotive is the only part of this still extant. The former railway booking hall, with its varnished woodwork, is now a tourist information office. Other features include a screen arch entrance similar to the one at London Paddington, French pavilion turrets, cherry red brickwork and a spacious cab yard with a graceful curved roof.

> **All Bar One, 40 Windsor Royal Station, Windsor, Berkshire, SL4 1PJ. Tel. 01753 857570.**
> **Daily 10am – midnight.**
> **www.allbarone.co.uk**

The Great Western in 2007.

WOLVERHAMPTON (LOW LEVEL), WEST MIDLANDS (station closed)

Former Great Western and Oxford, Worcester & Wolverhampton Railways, joint main line from London (Paddington) to Birkenhead and other destinations.

THE GREAT WESTERN

Set on a cobbled street corner, this railway-themed, real ale honey-pot is opposite the old station, where Castles, Kings and Halls once paused with their trains of chocolate-and-cream carriages. Built in the 1850s and Grade II listed, the pub has survived with a group of other railway buildings despite many changes in the vicinity. A long established outlet for Bathams and Holdens beers (including mild) and changing guest ales. Customers entering the quarry-tiled front bar find the counter decorated with 'Beware of the Trains' and 'Booking Office' signs and a *faux* GWR-style canopy. The railway theme continues in the long lounge with its bench seating, leading to a conservatory and small outdoor area. There are enamel and cast-iron signs, lamps, prints, a veritable gallery of steam-era photographs and some token block signalling equipment. Open fires complete the cosy ambience. There is also ephemera of Wolverhampton Wanderers FC: the pub is busy when the team is at home.

With two friends, I chose the Western to begin a memorable crawl of Black Country pubs by train and bus. Catching a morning train from London Euston, we visited eight hostelries, including three brewery taps, and were back in the capital well before closing time. The fact that three 'southerners' had chosen Wolverhampton as a day trip destination was a source of much merriment to the regulars. Meals, sometimes including the local delicacy 'grey peas and bacon', are served until 3pm. To walk to the pub from Wolverhampton Station, use the subway beside the main entrance and turn right at the end.

The former station: Has a Grade II listed frontage, in Italianate style and of blue engineering brick, as imposing as when opened in 1854. The last express to London Paddington left in 1967, the station closing to passenger traffic in 1972 though it survived as a parcels depot until 1981. The area once occupied by platform and tracks now contains residential accommodation and a hotel.

> **The Great Western, Sun Street, Wolverhampton,**
> **West Midlands, WV10 0DJ. Tel. 01902 351090.**
> **Daily 11am – 11pm (Sunday 10.30pm).**

WORKSOP, NOTTINGHAMSHIRE

Former Manchester Sheffield & Lincolnshire Railway (GCR) between Sheffield and Retford and terminus of the Robin Hood line from Nottingham.

THE MALLARD

The diminutive size of The Mallard is in direct contrast to its popularity. Once an ordinary buffet of the type that graced hundreds of station platforms, it has long been established as an independently run pub, with a well-deserved reputation for real ale and a wide selection of continental bottled beers. My first visit was before the smoking ban and it didn't need too many cigarette-wielding customers to create an atmosphere like an engine shed in steam days. Smoky pubs are now a distant memory and you can enjoy a fog-free pint here in close company with fellow drinkers. There are normally three ales and these change regularly. A micro-brewery planned for the cellar, called Double Top, finally opened in 2012 and its beer names are darts themed. On my early evening visit, a combination of locals and rail

The sign at Worksop Station says it all!

travellers were enjoying the ambience. Though only 13 people, it seemed like a crowd in this cosy spot. Numerous awards from the local CAMRA branch are on show, and real ale newsletters and rail timetables displayed. No meals are served but fresh cobs are available daily. Children are not allowed; dogs welcome.

The main station building, in Jacobean style and of honey-coloured stone, is Grade II listed. It dates from 1849 with early twentieth century additions. A decorative entranceway and hexagonal chimney-stacks lend the look of an historic house. This grandeur is a result of railway patronage by the dukes of Newcastle and Portland, hailing from Clumber Park and Welbeck Abbey respectively. The building containing the pub is plainer, though it retains saw-tooth chimney-pots and platform awning. Worksop East signal box, beside the level crossing, dates from 1880 and is wood-built with 'herringbone' gables.

Nearby: In Blyth Grove, a half-a-mile away, is a time capsule. Mr Straw's House is an ordinary Edwardian semi but its interior is filled with household objects spanning a century. The frugal Straw family ensured that time stood still in the 1920s. As a small National Trust property, advance booking is required, tel. 01909 482380.

> **The Mallard, Station Approach, Carlton Road, Worksop, Nottinghamshire, S81 7AG. Tel. 07973 521824. Daily noon – 11pm (Monday opens 5pm, Sunday closes 10.30pm).**

WYLAM, NORTHUMBERLAND

Former Newcastle & Carlisle Railway (NER) between Newcastle upon Tyne and Carlisle.

THE BOATHOUSE

George Stephenson, the 'father of railways', was born in Wylam, though there's no record of him slaking his thirst at this hostelry. Situated conveniently opposite the station and beside a level crossing, it's no wonder this is the unofficial waiting room. A few yards away, a Meccano-like gantry signal box built by the North Eastern Railway in 1897 and Grade II listed, is a striking feature straddling the main line.

A sign outside proclaims 'Arguably the best pub in the world.' With 14 hand-pumps and several accolades as CAMRA regional pub of the year, it is certainly a contender. The wide selection of delicious ales, like Nel's Best and Matfen Magic from Newcastle's High House Farm Brewery, is complemented by an ever-changing range from other micro-breweries in the North East. Examples from Allendale and Mordue, plus Houston from Scotland, were offered on my visit; also a choice of farmhouse ciders. Meals served daily, all afternoon. The main bar has a flag-stoned floor, oak beams, a large fireplace with blazing fire in winter and is furnished with old sewing machine tables, upholstered benches and farmhouse chairs. Historical photos, Pub of the Year certificates and a plethora of pump-clips and bottles complete the decoration. There is also a lounge with juke-box. Stained glass is set into the bar doors. Regular bank holiday beer festivals.

Nearby: Across the River Tyne, the stone-built miner's cottage where George Stephenson was born in 1781 is maintained by the National Trust and furnished in period style. A riverside path follows the former Wylam Colliery wagonway. The station house is now converted to offices though passengers can still use the stone-built waiting shelter.

> **The Boathouse, Station Road, Wylam, Northumberland, NE41 8HR. Tel. 01661 853431. Daily 11am – 11pm (Sunday noon – 11pm). www.boathousewylam.info**

The Boathouse, with diesel unit 142 084 passing under the signal box at Wylam on its way to Newcastle on 30 June, 2007.

WYMONDHAM, NORFOLK

Former Norfolk Railway (GER) between Norwich and Ely and junction for Dereham (via Mid-Norfolk Railway, a heritage line).

STATION BISTRO (LICENSED, NO REAL ALE)

Nineteen high-back seats from British Railways carriages, complete with LNER antimacassars, pendant lamps and luggage racks, fill the 'railway room' of this family-run establishment occupying the station building. With a little daydreaming, diners can imagine themselves on the 'Flying Scotsman' or 'Eastern Counties Express' while tucking into home-made cakes or supping an espresso coffee. The surrounding historical photographs of the station, and stills from the film classic *Brief Encounter,* complete the nostalgic idyll. On cooler days, there is a fire blazing in the hearth, too.

I first found this place in 2006, stepping off a train on a baking July afternoon. Baskets brimming with flowers hung from the awning, wires controlling the semaphore signals whispered beside the tracks and the station was immaculate. This establishment was then called Brief Encounter and filled with railway memorabilia, a labour of love for David Turner who rescued and restored the run-down junction station in 1989, partly as a piano showroom. Mr Turner retired in early 2011 and most of the railway paraphernalia was removed. The baton was handed over to the Pilgrim family who are determined to develop and improve the food offering. There are still items to interest rail fans, including a wealth of local, steam-era photographs. Wood partitioning from the booking office, with its sliding ticket window, is *in situ* and the GER waiting room table of 1883 is used by diners. Three large gas lamps, converted to electricity, hang from the ceiling.

Cooked breakfasts are served until late morning, followed by lunch with daily specials, including roasts on Sundays, until 2.30pm. Light snacks, homemade cakes and desserts are served all day. There is no draught beer but bottled ales are from Adnams

The entrance to the refreshment room at Wymondham in 2006, when it was called Brief Encounter.

and Greene King. Wine is sold by the glass and bottle and a choice of teas and filter coffee is served. The brick-and-flint station building in which the Bistro is situated dates from 1845. It once had a staff of thirty and sports a distinctive flat awning with valancing, matched on the opposite platform whose building is also intact. A weather-boarded signal box, painted green and cream, stands proudly to the west of the station and a semaphore signal is preserved in the yard: this should survive when the main-line semaphores are eventually removed.

Nearby: Excursion trains still occasionally run onto a branch north to Dereham, closed to passengers in 1969. This is now the Mid-Norfolk Railway, whose vintage diesel and occasional steam services depart from Wymondham Abbey, less than a mile away. There are plans to extend them from Dereham to County School, closed as a through route (to Wells) since 1964 but now restored, with a refreshment room. Wymondham is an attractive town known for its abbey church and market cross.

Station Bistro, Station Road, Wymondham, Norfolk, NR18 0ZJ. Tel. 01953 606433. Daily 8.30am – 5pm. Fri/Sat 6 – 9pm. www.station-bistro-wymondham.co.uk

YORK, NORTH YORKSHIRE

Former North Eastern Railway (LNER) main line between Doncaster and Thirsk and other routes.

YORK TAP

One of the most delightful on-station survivors of the Edwardian era, the NER's ornate, Art Nouveau tea room of 1906 returned to its original role as a place of refreshment – as a 'craft beer house' – in 2011. Designed by the company's chief architect William Bell, it ceased as a tea-room decades ago, serving as home to a 'Rail Riders' club for youngsters, then setting for York model railway. Now leased to Pivovar, the company behind the Sheffield and Euston Taps (q.v.) has led an ambitious restoration in collaboration with the Railway Heritage Trust.

The wooden exterior has been restored to its Edwardian colours, complete with stained glass upper panes. Interior highlights include hand-made Tiffany pendant lights, a polished terrazzo floor, restored fire surrounds and an ornate plaster ceiling. The plaster details, which had largely disintegrated, were replicated using moulds from the originals. The ceiling features two leaded stained glass domes, one of which is original and the other a reproduction. A mahogany island bar, inspired by one which once graced Swindon's original GWR refreshment rooms, has been custom-built. A revolving entrance door is an antique rescued from another building. Ale aficionados can choose from 18 real ales, 12 craft keg beers and a wide range of foreign bottled ones. There is a choice of cask ciders. A framed period photograph of the original tea-room allows comparison of old

and new incarnations. There is 'outside' seating on the platform.

The station: Built to replace an original terminus, it was completed in 1877 and built, like Newcastle, on a curve. Sheltered by a magnificent train-shed of iron and glass, each of its three arched spans is almost eight hundred feet long. Look for the replica 'zero milepost' of pre-grouping railway companies that served the city, providing an array of liveries. Beside the footbridge, a wooden former signal-box stands 15 feet above the platform and now serves as a coffee shop with a difference, its entrance beneath a large, triple-faced clock.

York Tap (adjacent to platform 3), Tea Room Square, Station Road, York, North Yorkshire, YO24 1AB. Tel. 01904 659009. Monday to Saturday 9am – midnight (Mon/Tues 11pm), Sunday 10am – 11.30pm. www.yorktap.com

The restored Edwardian tea-room at York, showing its island bar and one of the ornate ceiling domes. See page 16 for an exterior view taken in 1906.

APPENDIX I
BREWERIES PRODUCING 'RAILWAY ALES'

THE NUMBER OF micro-breweries in Britain has grown exponentially over the last four decades. According to beer writer Roger Protz, there are more than 700, four times as many as when CAMRA was launched in 1971 (*What's Brewing, April 2011, page 6*). This expansion has spawned a vast number of ales, each with its own distinctive taste. Underlining the fact that railways and beer go together so well, many enlightened brewers have given their brews railway oriented names. Sometimes this is because they have a historic link with railways, more often they simply like trains. These ales are worth seeking out, though some are brewed only occasionally.

As beers come and go, and new breweries are opening up constantly, this cannot be a definitive list. The author will be pleased to hear of other railway themed beers discovered by readers.

Ales are listed by brewery. Tasting notes are those provided by the brewery, except those marked with an asterisk, which are by the author. All beers are available in draught (cask) form only, unless 'bottled' or 'bottle conditioned' is stated, in which case it is available in cask and bottle. Many of these breweries welcome visitors and/or have on-site shops but readers are advised to contact them first to check.

ABV = Alcohol by Volume.

ADUR

Velocity, 4.4% ABV. Celebrates the LNER A4 Pacific locomotive *Mallard,* which holds the world speed record for a steam locomotive of 126 mph, achieved in July 1938. The label includes an impressionistic illustration of the engine (in green livery) at speed. First brewed during a spell of hot weather, it fermented faster than the high gravity beers brewer Andy Dwelly was experimenting with at the time, inspiring the name. A traditional bitter with Perle and Hallertauer hops. Fresh flavour, at the lower end of the bitterness scale, with a hint of marmalade. Bottle conditioned.

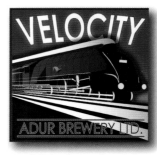

A five-and-a-half barrel brewery established in the Adur Valley, Sussex in 2008, run as a co-operative since 2011.

Mouse Lane, Steyning, West Sussex, BN44 3DG. Tel. 01273 467527. www.adurvalleycop.com

BEER ENGINE, THE

Piston Bitter, 4.3% ABV. A mid-brown, sweet-tasting beer with a pleasant, bittersweet aftertaste.

Rail Ale, 3.8% ABV. A straw coloured beer with a fruity aroma and a sweet, fruity finish.

0-4-0 Shunter, 4% ABV. Amber coloured with a hoppy, sweet aftertaste.

Silver Bullet, 4% ABV. The brewery's 25th anniversary ale. Pump clip shows a New York Central streamlined Hudson locomotive, as used on the 'Twentieth Century Limited'. A clean, pale brew with a hoppy sweet aftertaste.

Sleeper Heavy, 5.4% ABV. A red coloured beer with a fruity, sweet taste and a bitter finish.

Celebrated its 25th year of brewing in 2008, making it Devon's oldest micro-brewery. Since 2005, run by Mike (a retired army chef) and Jan Tutty. Based in the eponymous pub, originally a railway hotel, hence the rail theme to the beers. Contact details, see Gazetteer (page 97).

BEWDLEY BREWERY

Black 5 Special, 3.8% ABV. Label shows a Black Five locomotive with passenger train. Produced for Severn Valley Railway. Pale amber colour, uses Worcestershire Goldings and Fuggles hops, giving a hoppy finish. Bottled.

Flying Pig, 3.8% ABV. Label depicts LMS 2-6-0 Class 4MT locomotive number 43106 *The Flying Pig*. Produced for Severn Valley Railway. Bottled only.

Peppercorn Pedigree, 4.1% ABV. Label depicts Peppercorn A1 pacific locomotive No. 60163 *Tornado*. Produced for Severn Valley Railway. Pale copper colour. Uses Worcestershire, Goldings and Fuggles hops. Sweeter, maltier beer with a slight hoppy finish. Bottled.

Started in 2008, the first brewery in Bewdley for 96 years. Other bottled ales produced for the SVR are **Hagley Hall** (3.8%), **Hinton Manor** (4.3%) and **2857** (5.0%).

Unit 7, Bewdley Craft Centre, Lax Lane, Bewdley, Worcestershire, DY12 2DZ. Tel. 01299 405148. www.bewdleybrewery.co.uk

BOX STEAM

Broad Gauge, 4.8% ABV. Premium bitter with delicate blackcurrant aroma. Gentle bitterness with subtle spicy notes and sweet fruit finish. First brewed April 2011.

Chuffin' Ale, 4% ABV. Traditional best bitter first brewed for 175th anniversary of the GWR. Chestnut colour, fruity aroma. Bottled.

Derail Ale, 5.2% ABV. Hoppy traditional India Pale Ale, full flavoured with an intense floral aroma, finished with a well balanced bitterness. Bottled.

Golden Bolt, 3.8% ABV. Named after a legend that a solid gold rivet bolt was used in the construction of Brunel's Royal Albert Bridge spanning the Tamar. Previously known as Revd Awdry's Ale in honour of the creator of *Thomas the Tank Engine*, but rebranded in 2009. A light, straw coloured ale with a hoppy aftertaste.

Piston Broke, 5.0% ABV. Single hopped golden beer with a hoppy aroma and a dry finish.

Tunnel Vision, 4.2% ABV. Inspired by Brunel's Box Tunnel. Copper coloured, clean tasting traditional bitter with a slight bitterness on the palate. Bottled.

Family run using a steam heated copper. Beer names are inspired by the life and works of Isambard Kingdom Brunel, whose Box Tunnel carries the London to Bristol ex-GWR main line through the hillside close to the original brewery site. Owns the Cross Guns at Avoncliff (see page 52).

The Midlands, Holt, Wiltshire BA14 6RU.
Tel. 01225 782700. www.boxsteambrewery.co.uk

BRUNSWICK

Midnight Express, 3.9% ABV. Brewed annually in May for CAMRA's Mild Ale promotion, this is a lightly hopped, dark Midlands mild, with plenty of wheat malt for body and mouth feel.

Railway Porter, 4.3% ABV. A traditional dark porter, lightly hopped with hints of coffee and chocolate.

Station Approach, 4.7% ABV. A finely balanced light coloured premium ale, with slight citrus and honey notes in the finish.

Brewery opened in 1991 in Derby's Brunswick Inn, part of the Everard's pub estate. Contact details, see Gazetteer (page 77).

BUNTINGFORD

92 Squadron, 4.5% ABV. Label shows Battle of Britain class 4-6-2 No. 34081 *92 Squadron*, designed by Bulleid for the Southern Railway, built in 1948 and returned to steam in 1998. A copper coloured bitter, using Amarillo hops brewed to support the Battle of Britain Locomotive Society which owns the locomotive, based on the North Norfolk Railway. Early bitterness leading to intense fruit notes*. Bottled.

Railway themed one-off beers (various names and strengths). The company has produced a large number of one-off brews, with attractive pump clips, many of which are quite collectible. In 2008 it did around 15, these days the number is reduced and it has moved away from railway-related artwork. Two ranges stand out, one named after BR Britannia Pacific locomotives, the other locomotives of the London & North Eastern Railway. Diesel themed beers have also been produced. Bottled only.

Western Champion, 4.2% ABV. Label shows the eponymous Western class diesel hydraulic D1015, built in the 1960s at Swindon works, now owned by the Diesel Traction Group, on a main-line excursion. A golden best bitter brewed with Pilgrim, Pioneer and Chinook hops. Refreshingly bitter but not too heavy, with a fruity aroma and aftertaste. Bottled.

Early production from 2001 and opened a 15-barrel plant in a converted barn in 2005. Members of the team maintain a railway interest and this is possibly the only brewery to have housed a five-inch gauge locomotive, a Western class diesel, and model railway, in the brewhouse.

Greys Brewhouse, Therfield Road, Royston,
Hertfordshire, SG8 9NW. Tel. 01763 250749.
www.buntingford-brewery.co.uk

BUTCOMBE

Brunel 200 IPA, 5% ABV. The brewery was asked by the Brunel 200 Committee to produce a beer to celebrate the 200th birthday of the engineer in 2006. It was planned to be a one off, but proved to be so popular that it has become a regular seasonal ale (September – November). A dry, hoppy, full bodied IPA with a bitter sweet finish. Bottled and cask.

Established in old farm buildings in Butcombe in 1978, the brewery moved to a purpose built plant south of Bristol in 2004.

Cox's Green, Wrington, Bristol,
BS40 5PA. Tel. 01934 863963.
www.butcombe.com

CALEDONIAN

Flying Scotsman, 4% ABV. Originally produced as a spring seasonal at 4.6% and launched as a permanent brand in 2011. The name is licensed by the National Museum of Science and Industry which owns the eponymous locomotive. Malty in aroma and balanced with a hint of raisin spiciness and toasted dryness. A fresh, slightly citrus tang leads to a rich, rounded finish. Bottled. Established in 1869, now part of Heineken UK.

42 Slateford Road, Edinburgh, EH11 1PH.
Tel. 0131 337 1286. www.caledonianbeer.com

COTLEIGH

GWR 175, 4.2% ABV. Created in 2010 to mark the GWR's 175th anniversary. Bright, golden beer, smooth and malty with a background honey flavour and citrus finish. Bottled.

Old Steamer, 4.2% ABV. Brewed for the West Somerset Railway, and bearing that heritage railway's logo. Uses Pale and Crystal malts and Goldings, Challenger and Styrian hops. A bright golden beer, smooth and malty with a background of honey flavour and a citrus smooth finish. Bottled only.

Established in 1979 in the stable block of a Tiverton farmhouse; expanded in 1985.

Ford Road, Wiveliscombe, Somerset, TA4 2RE. Tel. 01984 624086. www.cotleighbrewery.com

COTTAGE

In addition to the following permanent, year-round beers, a new train themed special is brewed approximately monthly but space does not permit these to be listed.

Broadgauge Bitter, 3.9% ABV. A light coloured session bitter, brewed with Progress, Challenger and Styrian Goldings hops; floral aroma and a balanced bitter finish.

Champflower Ale, 4.2% ABV. Wyke Champflower was a locality on the Somerset & Dorset Joint Railway. Light chestnut in colour and well balanced; lingering bitter finish.

Golden Arrow, 4.5% ABV. A light golden colour with a distinctive floral hop flavour and aroma. Silver medal winner at CAMRA's Great British Beer Festival.

Goldrush, 5.0% ABV. A deep golden ale, brewed with Cascade hops, well balanced, crisp and refreshing. Champion strong ale and supreme champion beer at the 13th SIBA Maltings beer festival.

Somerset & Dorset Ale, 4.4% ABV. A well hopped, malty beer with a deep red colour.

Southern Bitter, 3.7% ABV. A light, copper coloured session bitter. Full bodied with a distinctive hop aroma and finish. Champion standard bitter at the 13th SIBA Maltings beer festival.

Founded in 1993 by Chris and Helen Norman at their home, but since relocated to a new building at Lovington near Castle Cary. A railway theme has

been a constant since the brewery's inception. While brewing his first beer, Chris crossed the track-bed of the Somerset & Dorset Joint Railway and decided it would be the name of his debut ale.

The Old Cheese Dairy, Hornblotton Road, Lovington, Castle Cary, Somerset, BA7 7PS. Tel. 01963 240551. www.cottagebrewing.co.uk

FOXFIELD

Brief Encounter, 3.8% ABV. First brewed for the Station pub at Ashton-under-Lyne. A very hoppy bitter using Goldings and Styrian Goldings varieties. Fruity with sweet balance and a long, bitter finish.

Brewery started in Wakefield, West Yorkshire (Tigertops) but an additional, purpose-built three-barrel plant at the Prince of Wales pub in Foxfield, Cumbria opened in 1997. Contact details, see Gazetteer (page 81).

FRODSHAM

Night Mail 4.7% ABV. Named in honour of the film *Night Mail* made in 1936 by the GPO Film Unit, with verse by W.H. Auden, illustrating the work of the railways in moving the mail. Brewer Barrie Davidson wrote a dissertation on the film for his degree and the beer's colour is 'black as night'.

A dry stout using roasted barley, oat malt and three hop addition. Sharp with mellow aftertaste. The pump clip depicts LMS Royal Scot locomotive 6115, *Scots Guardsman*, now preserved. Bottled.

Began in 2005 as Stationhouse Brewery, the name originating from a plan to open in the Grade II listed station house at Frodsham, which did not materialise.

Lady Heyes Craft Centre, Kingsley Road, Frodsham, Cheshire, WA6 6SU. Tel. 01928 787917. www.frodshambrewery.co.uk

GOFF'S

Rail Ale, 4.7% ABV. A light coloured, well-hopped ale, brewed and bottled for the Gloucestershire Warwickshire Railway. Label shows Modified Hall class locomotive No. 7903 *Foremarke Hall*. Bottled only.

A family run Cotswold micro-brewery established in 1994.

9 Isbourne Way, Winchcombe, Gloucestershire, GL54 5NS. Tel. 01242 603383. www.goffsbrewery.com

GREAT OAKLEY

Welland Valley Mild, 3.6% ABV. Pump clip depicts the Midland Railway's Harringworth Viaduct of 1879, the country's longest (apart from urban ones in South London) at

1,275 yards, crossing the eponymous valley on 82 arches. Dark, traditional mild, with a slight roast taste. First brewed in 2006 for the Welland Valley Beer Festival.

Established 2005 by Phil and Hazel Greenway, who run the five-barrel plant. Brewery tap is the Malt Shovel Tavern, Northampton.

Bridge Farm, 11 Brooke Road, Great Oakley, near Corby, Northamptonshire, NN18 8HG. Tel. 01536 744888. www.greatoakleybrewery.co.uk

GREENFIELD

Black Five, 4% ABV. Nick-name of LMS Stanier 4-6-0 Class 5 locomotive, of which more than 800 were built from 1934-51. The beer is served on some railtours. Full flavoured dark bitter with a hint of liquorice. Creamy head, liquorice nose and light roast taste, with other flavours including chocolate and toffee*.

Delph Donkey, 4.1% ABV. Nick-name of a passenger train in Greater Manchester which ran from Oldham to Delph via Greenfield. The service was withdrawn in 1955 and Delph station closed. Golden beer with a floral aroma, lingering citrus

flavours, vanilla notes and a dry finish*.

Rail Ale, 4.2% ABV. The company's Dobcross Bitter rebadged for sale on Retro Rail Tours.

All the above are available bottle conditioned and cask. Established 2002 by a group of friends including Peter Percival, the brewer, who is a steam enthusiast.

Unit 8, Waterside Mills, Greenfield, Saddleworth, OL3 7NH. Tel. 01457 879789. www.greenfieldrealale.co.uk

HEPWORTH & CO.

Iron Horse, 4.8% ABV. The label shows Richard Trevithick's Coalbrookdale locomotive, *circa* 1803. Ruby coloured pale ale with a good head and hop nose, full of flavour including toffee and caramel notes*. Bottled.

Pullman, 4.2% ABV. The label shows Pullman car *Ibis*, built in 1925 by Birmingham Railway Carriage and Wagon Company, used on the 'Golden Arrow' in 1928 and boat train services between London and Southampton (1952). Acquired for the British Pullman of the 'Venice Simplon-Orient-Express' in 1981. Bitter using Sussex barley malt and hops. Copper coloured with a lasting head. Good hop nose and full bodied bitterness with cereal and walnut flavours and long hop finish*. Bottled.

Brewery is situated in a railway goods yard with its own platform and tracks. The beers are served regularly on the 'Venice Simplon-Orient-Express' and Bluebell Railway. The company logo is based on the British Railways 'totem' sign.

Chipman House, Nightingale Road, Horsham, West Sussex, RH12 2NW. Tel. 01403 269696. www.hepworthbrewery.co.uk

HESKET NEWMARKET

Ratty Ale, 4.3% ABV. Fine, smooth, malty beer. Brewed for the Ravenglass and Eskdale narrow gauge railway. The label depicts the 2-6-2 locomotive *Northern Rock*, which entered service in 1976. Bottle conditioned.

Established in 1988 in a converted barn at the Old Crown pub in Hesket Newmarket, Cumbria. Run as a community co-operative since 1999.

Old Crown Barn, Hesket Newmarket, Cumbria, CA7 8JG. Tel. 016974 78066. www.hesketbrewery.co.uk

HOBSONS

Manor Ale, 4.2% ABV. An amber beer, light, golden and hoppy with a citrus nose and zesty taste. Brewed for the Severn Valley Railway to celebrate its GWR 4-6-0 78xx Manor Class steam engines, one of which features on the label. Bottle conditioned.

Established in 1993.

Newhouse Farm, Tenbury Road, Cleobury Mortimer, Shropshire, DY14 8RD. Tel. 01299 270837. www.hobsons-brewery.co.uk

HUMPTY DUMPTY

Cheltenham Flyer, 4.6% ABV. Amber ale with a hint of malt and dry hop bitterness. In 1932 the Great Western Railway's express of this name became the first scheduled run above 70 mph to appear in a British timetable. The pump clip features the artwork of John Austin FGRA, showing the express making a spirited departure from the city. Bottle conditioned and cask.

Golden Gorse, 5.4% ABV. A finely balanced, premium pale golden ale with a fruity sweetness on the nose which is overtaken by a rush of Cascade hops, with a pleasant bitter aftertaste. Bottle conditioned.

Humpty Dumpty Porter, 5.4% ABV. Also known as Reedham Porter. London style porter using chocolate and black malts. Full roast aroma with hints of liquorice and a dry, bitter finish. Full body with coffee and chocolate notes delicately highlighted by a late addition of Fuggles hop. CAMRA East Anglia Champion Porter 2008. The pump clip, by artist Cherry Burns, depicts a porter at work on Reedham Station while a barmaid daydreams in the refreshment room. Bottle conditioned.

Little Sharpie, 3.8% ABV. Golden bitter with subtle grapefruit and lemon notes combining with light hoppiness to create a refreshing session beer*. 2009 CAMRA Champion Beer of Britain (Bronze Medal, Bitter). 'Sharpie' was the nick-name for locomotives built by Sharp-Stewart; the Little Sharpies were 2-4-0 mixed traffic engines designed by Charles Beyer for the Great Eastern Railway and introduced 1867-72. The engine depicted on the pump-clip is an artist's impression. Bottle conditioned.

Nord Atlantic, 3.7% ABV. Dark session bitter introduced in 2011, with crystal malt and strong hop character using Target and Challenger. Art Nouveau style pump clip with an impressionist depiction of a French Railways' Class 221 Atlantic (4-4-2) locomotive, as introduced in 1900 at the Paris World Fair.

Poppy Line Ale, 4.1% ABV. Brewed for the North Norfolk Railway. Bottled.

Railway Sleeper, 5.0% ABV. A full bodied, strong ale with a reddish brown hue, in which the nose is predominately fruity; long lasting dry finish. A rich, complex beer and one of the author's favourites. The pump clip depicts a freelance 4-6-0 locomotive, *Humpty Dumpty,* passing a windmill and typical Broadland boats. Bottle conditioned.

Swingbridge Stout, 4.1% ABV. Dark stout with a fine balance of roast and hoppy notes and a pale brown, creamy head. Brewed with dark malts, roasted barley and a small addition of oats. Punches above its relatively low gravity.

Named after the Reedham Swingbridge, the pump clip features artwork by Derrick Buck. Bottle conditioned.

The King John, 4.4% ABV. Full bodied amber IPA with lots of late hop goodness. The pump clip features artwork by John Austin FGRA of *King John,* King class locomotive number 6026, built in 1930, working a westbound express on the former GWR main line near Dawlish, Devon. Mr Austin, a real ale lover, frequents the Railwayman's Arms, Bridgnorth (q.v.), which he calls 'the best pub in Britain'. Bottle conditioned.

The brewery's name is taken from the nick-name for a class of 2-4-0 locomotive designed by James Holden for the Great Eastern Railway. It began in 1998 in stables at the rear of the Railway Tavern, Reedham. Subsequent owners (since 2006) are continuing the railway theme at a different village location.

Church Road, Reedham, Norwich, Norfolk, NR13 3TZ. Tel. 01493 701818. www.humptydumptybrewery.co.uk

IRONBRIDGE

Steam, 4.7% ABV. A winter seasonal. A 'California Common' beer style, with malty fruitiness and a pleasant lingering bitterness. Auburn colour with a creamy head. Uses Northdown and Challenger hops. Inspired by Richard Trevithick's Coalbrookdale locomotive of *circa* 1803 which appears on the pump clip.

Established in the Ironbridge Gorge in 2007.

Unit 7, Merrythought, The Wharfage, Ironbridge, Shropshire, TF8 7NJ. Tel. 01952 433910. http://ironbridgebrewery.co.uk

ITCHEN VALLEY

Watercress Line Bitter, 4.2% ABV. Seasonal (winter) beer. A hint of watercress gives this smooth bitter a unique flavour. Named after the Mid-Hants. heritage railway.

Founded in 1997 and based near the Mid-Hants. Railway.

Unit D, Prospect Commercial Park, New Alresford, Hampshire, SO24 9QF. Tel. 01962 735111. www.itchenvalley.com

KINVER

Light Railway, 3.8% ABV. A light, hoppy bitter. Pump clip depicts tramcar number 51 on the Kinver Light Railway which closed in 1930. Many of the brewery's other beers are named after local landmarks and attractions.

Five barrel brewery established in 2004.

Kinver Brewery Company, Unit 2, Fairfield Drive, Kinver, Stourbridge, West Midlands, DY7 6EW. Tel. 0771 584 2679. www.kinverbrewery.co.uk

MALLINSONS

Station Best Bitter, 4.2% ABV. Pale gold with a citrus hop aroma, bitter hop taste and finish. Bottle conditioned.

Viaduct Series, ABV varies. Series of limited production beers named after railway structures, such as Lydgate (Todmorden Viaduct) at 4.1% ABV.

Established in 2008 in a Huddersfield garage by former school teacher Tara Mallinson.

Plover Road Garage, Plover Road, Lindley, Huddersfield, HD3 3HS. Tel. 01484 654301. www.drinkmallinsons.co.uk

RCH

Double Header, 5.3% ABV. A golden brew made with pale ale malt and Goldings hops, giving a well balanced, hoppy flavour. Bottle conditioned.

Firebox, 6% ABV. A reddish-brown coloured strong bitter with a combination of citrus hops and cherry fruit bittersweet flavours, giving a dry, bitter finish. Bottle conditioned.

There is also a rolling programme of 14 monthly cask specials including:

Steamed Flames, 4.5% ABV. A golden beer with Bramling Cross and North Downs hops producing citrus and blackcurrant flavours.

Steam Lovers, 4.7% ABV. A golden beer using North Downs hops.

Steam Showers, 4.8% ABV. A rich, gold beer using Fuggles and Bramling Cross hops.

Steam Special, 5% ABV. Pump clip depicts ex-GWR Prairie tank number 4160, now in preservation. A well-balanced, hoppy beer using Bramling Cross and Goldings hops.

Paul Davey and Graham Dunbaven, co-owner and brewer respectively, are railway enthusiasts and their brewery is adjacent to the ex-GWR main line between Weston-super-Mare and Bristol.

West Hewish, Weston-super-Mare, North Somerset, BS24 6RR. Tel. 01934 834447. www.rchbrewery.com

RICHMOND

Station Ale, 4% ABV. A light golden coloured bitter using pale and crystal malts with English hedgerow hops. Bottle conditioned and cask.

A six barrel microbrewery established in 2008 in the Grade II* listed former York & Newcastle Railway station building of 1846 (closed in 1969). The Station, recipient of an Ian Allan Heritage award in 2009, also houses a cinema, bar/bistro and retail outlets.

The Station Brewery, Richmond, North Yorkshire, DL10 4LD. Tel. 01748 828266. www.richmondbrewing.co.uk

ROSSENDALE

Railway Sleeper, 4.2% ABV. Amber coloured, bitter, hoppy beer. Brewed in response to a request from regulars at Stockport's Railway Inn (hence the name) for an extremely hoppy, bitter ale. A favourite of the author, though not brewed since 2011.

The brewery opened in 1994 at the Griffin Inn at Haslingden, Lancashire. Sales are limited to a small tied estate in the Greater Manchester area.

Griffin Inn, 84-86 Hud Rake, Haslingden, BB4 5AF. Tel. 01706 214021. www.rossendalebrewery.co.uk

ROTHER VALLEY

The following seasonal beers are brewed and bottled exclusively for the Kent & East Sussex Railway.

Dad's Delight, 4.3% ABV. For Father's Day (June). The label carries a photograph of the tank locomotive *Bodiam* and the railway's insignia.

Levers Alone, 4.3% ABV. The label shows a cartoon of a signalman at work in his box.

Santa Special, 4.4% ABV. The label carries a cartoon of Santa Claus on his sleigh, attached to a tank locomotive with the letters 'K&ESR' spelled out in smoke.

Established in Northiam in 1993 adjacent to a hop farm overlooking the River Rother on the Kent and East Sussex border (see page 37).

Gate Court Farm, Station Road, Northiam, East Sussex, TN31 6QT. Tel. 07798 877551.

SAMBROOK'S

Junction, 4.5% ABV. Named after the local station, Clapham Junction. Deep amber ale brewed with Challenger, Bramling Cross and Goldings hops, giving a spicy hop character.

Brewery established by a former managing director of Ringwood Brewery and city accountant in 2008.

Units 1 and 2, Yelverton Road, Battersea, SW11 3QG.
Tel: 0207 228 0598.
www.sambrooksbrewery.co.uk

SNOWDONIA

WHB (Welsh Highland Bitter) 5.2% ABV. Signature ale named after the narrow-gauge railway running yards from the brewery. Pump-clip depicts a 2-6-2+2-6-2T Garratt locomotive built by Beyer Peacock in Manchester in 1958 and returned from service in South Africa for the WHR. Balanced in bitterness and malt body, extends to produce a rich, semi-sweet finish. Uses Crystal malt, giving a biscuit, toffee note.

Carmen's Pulling Power, 4.8% ABV. Brewed occasionally, first for the 2010 WHR Rail Ale Festival. Pump clip depicts a Garratt locomotive carrying a battery lamp. All malt brew using Challenger and Fuggles hops. A dark, ebony ale with a creamy head and more than a hint of liquorice. Looks like a porter but tastes more like a bitter*.

The main outlet is the brewery itself, the Snowdonia Park, based in a former stationmaster's house on the Welsh Highland Railway. The brewer is Carmen Pierce, who crafts ales with mountain water in the basement of this remote pub; see Gazetteer (page 116).

STONEHOUSE

Station Bitter, 3.9% ABV. Amber coloured, full bodied session

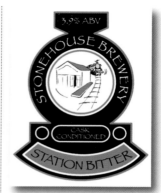

beer with a blend of hops and roasted malt.

Cambrian Gold, 4.2% ABV. A golden, fruity beer with a subtle, dry finish.

Wheeltappers, 4.5% ABV. A golden wheat beer with hints of coriander and lemon zest.

Off the Rails, 4.8% ABV. A rich and malty premium bitter with plenty of hop flavour.

Kingston Flyer KPA, 4.6% ABV. Kiwi Pale Ale named after New Zealand's vintage steam train operation on the southern shores of Lake Wakatipu. Brewed with Green Bullet hops from New Zealand for a distinctive herby, floral note.

All beers have a railway theme and are available in cask and bottle. The pump clips and labels are shaped like the head-on profile of a steam locomotive. A family run brewery adjacent to the former Cambrian Railways. (The Cambrian Heritage Railways project, at nearby Llynclys South Station, is restoring part of the main line.)

Weston, Oswestry, Shropshire, SY10 9ES. Tel. 01691 676457. www.stonehousebrewery.co.uk

TRING

Signal Box, 4.1% ABV. Brown ale named after the Midland Railway signal-box at St Albans (City), dating from 1892. After closure in 1979 it was listed, then restored by the St Albans Signal Box Preservation Trust which opens it to the public. A malty, full-bodied brew with a gentle bitterness and late hop aroma. Last brewed October 2010; may be revived as a seasonal.

Founded in 1992 by Richard

Shardlow, previously brewer at Greene King, Ruddles and Devenish, joined in 2000 by Andrew Jackson, ex-Whitbread.

Dunsley Farm, London Road, Tring, Hertfordshire, HP23 6HA. Tel. 01442 890721. www.tringbrewery.co.uk

WARCOP COUNTRY ALES

Caspa Lager, 5.4% ABV. Bill Picton was brewing his first lager, using American Liberty hops, when members of the Crewe and Shrewsbury Passenger Association visited – hence the name. A light, golden beer with hints of grapefruit and pineapple, a roast bitterness and dry finish*. Conditioned and stored in casks for two months before bottling. Bottled.

Shunters, 5.4% ABV. A golden, strong ale using Fuggles hops for a subtle floral aroma. Brewed occasionally. Bottled.

A family run brewery established in 1999 in a former milking parlour.

9 Nellive Park, St Brides, Wentloog, Gwent, NP10 8SE. Tel. 01633 680058. www.warcopales.com

WICKWAR

I.K.B., 4.5% ABV. Named in honour of I. K. Brunel and showing the great engineer and his Clifton Suspension Bridge on the pump clip. A ruby red beer with strong multimalt flavours, balanced by a rich fruit character and aromatic, dry finish. Uses Cascade, Challenger and Fuggles hops. Bottled.

Station Porter, 6.1% ABV. A smooth, dark ruby porter with aromas of roasted malt, coffee and spiced fruit. CAMRA Supreme Champion Winter Beer of Britain 2008. Bottled.

Established in 1990, brews in an original brewery building dating from the 1860s, adjacent to the site of Wickwar Station on the former Bristol & Gloucester Railway.

Station Road, Wickwar, Gloucestershire, GL12 8NB. Tel. 01454 299592. www.wickwarbrewing.co.uk

WOLD TOP

A4 Amber, 4.4% ABV. First brewed in 2007 for a LNER Festival on the North Yorkshire Moors Railway. Pump clip shows an artist's impression of an A4 Gresley Pacific No. 60009 *Amber* (the number carried in reality by *Union of South Africa*) in blue livery. Fruity and light with a dry finish, it uses Maris Otter malt with Goldings, Styrian and Cascade hops. Last brewed in 2010.

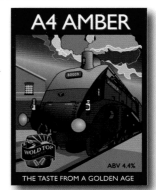

Farm based brewery established in 2003 using chalk filtered water from its own borehole.

Hunmanby Grange, Wold Newton, Driffield, East Yorkshire, YO25 3HS. Tel. 01723 892222. www.woldtopbrewery.co.uk

WOLF

Railway themed ales (various strengths). Four ales brewed for the North Norfolk Railway, sold separately and as a four-bottle gift pack. **Marriott's Revenge** (3.9% ABV) marking the re-instatement of Sheringham level crossing after a gap of 46 years and showing a BR Britannia Class Pacific locomotive; **Little Black Goods** (4.5% ABV) showing an LNER J15 Class; **Wandering 1500** (3.7% ABV) showing an LNER B12 Class; and **Austerity Ale** (4.7% ABV) showing an 'Austerity' 2-10-0. Bottled.

Opened in 1995 on the former Gaymers Cider site, which it outgrew, ten years later opening a new, purpose-built brewery and bottling plant in a nearby village.

Rookery Farm, Silver Street, Besthorpe, Attleborough, Norfolk, NR17 2LD. Tel. 01953 457775. www.wolfbrewery.com

WYLAM

Locomotion No. 1, 5% ABV. Matured at one degree Celcius for three weeks in the tradition of a lagered continental beer. Made with lager and Vienna malts, a lager yeast and the Saaz hop. Bottled.

Puffing Billy, 4.7% ABV. A brown ale named after William Hedley's locomotive of 1813. No longer brewed.

Rocket, 5% ABV. A multi award winning pale copper coloured best bitter named after the locomotive built by George and Robert Stephenson in 1829 for the Rainhill Trials. Fresh citrus and aromatic character from Centennial hops, with a bitter finish. Bottled.

Whistle Stop, 4.4% ABV. A complex amber ale, brewed for the Whistle Stop Initiative (Newcastle to Carlisle line). Last brewed 2008.

Established in a former dairy farm near Wylam in 2000, a larger plant was opened in a converted barn six years later. Wylam was birthplace of railway pioneer George Stephenson.

South Houghton Farm, Heddon on the Wall,
Northumberland, NE15 0EZ. Tel. 01661 853377.
www.wylambrewery.co.uk

A hand-pump in use in the kitchen car of a Welsh Highland train in 2010.

APPENDIX II
EVENTS CALENDAR

WHAT COULD BE better than enjoying a real ale or cider in an atmospheric railway setting or on board a steam train? The following is a month-by-month guide to special events that successfully combine the twin delights. It is not intended to be comprehensive and, like all events, especially those dependent on voluntary help, they are subject to change or cancellation. Readers are advised to check, using the contact details provided, before making any travel plans.

CAMRA = Organized or supported by the Campaign for Real Ale. All locations are Heritage Railways except those marked *

FEBRUARY

R.A.T. (Real Ale Train) on the Mid-Hants Railway (Watercress Line). First train of the season, then runs one to three times a month until December. Makes two round trips from Alton to Alresford with draught ales from up to two local breweries on board. Advance booking essential. Tel. 01962 733810. www.watercressline.co.uk

*Derby Winter Beer Festival (CAMRA). Held since 2011 in a Grade II listed, former Midland Railway roundhouse, restored as part of Derby College campus. Possibly the world's oldest surviving roundhouse (1839), it is a perfect setting (tours may be available). The city is known for its wide range of pubs. www.derbycamra.org.uk

MARCH

*Chappel Winter Beer Festival (CAMRA), East Anglian Railway Museum. The first winter festival was held in 2010 in this evocative railway setting beside Chappel & Wakes Colne Station, Essex. Advance booking for evening sessions. Tel. 01206 242524. www.chappelbeerfestival.org.uk/winter

*Manchester MOSI Real Ale Festival (CAMRA). Held in the Power Hall of the Museum of Science and Industry, surrounded by railway locomotives and working engines. First staged in 2011, the organizers intend it to be an annual event. Liverpool Road, Manchester M3 4F. www.thcamra.org.uk

APRIL

Rail Ale Train, Bluebell Railway. First ale train of the season (there are usually three per year, others in June and August) between Kingscote (or East Grinstead) and Sheffield Park Draught ales carried on board, with stops en route for further refreshment. An evening of steam, real ale and jazz, with a choice of guest beers. Advance booking essential. Tel. 01825 720800. www.bluebell-railway.co.uk

Steam, Beer and Jazz Special, Bodmin & Wenford Railway. First of several beer and jazz trains run during the season. Band plays at Bodmin Station, with the musical entertainment continuing on board a train with real ale bar. Booking essential. Tel. 01208 73555. www.bodminandwenfordrailway.co.uk.

MAY

Beer Festival and Diesel Gala, Swanage Railway. Heritage diesels in action, combined with the Dorset Beer Festival at Harman's Cross. Tel. 01929 425800. www.swanagerailway.co.uk

Rail Ale Festival (CAMRA), Barrow Hill Roundhouse, near Chesterfield. Held in the country's last operational roundhouse on a 16-acre site with a fine collection of locomotives. Opened in 1870 by the Midland Railway, in its heyday more than 200 enginemen would sign-on here daily to take out coal trains. Grade II listed, it is run by Barrow Hill Engine Shed Society. The festival marked its tenth anniversary in 2011. A free bus from Chesterfield usually operates. Tel. 01246 472450. www.barrowhill.org

Rail and Ale Excursion, Llangollen Railway. First ale excursion of the season (there are approximately eight annually, until December). Hauled by a vintage steam engine, each special makes two return evening journeys alongside the River Dee to Carrog (total 32 miles), carrying up to ten ales, mainly from local independent brewers. Service began with two ale trains in 2008; they regularly sell-out. Advance booking is essential. Also mini festivals at the spring and autumn steam galas. Tel. 01978 860979. www.llangollen-railway.co.uk

Real Ale Festival, Isle of Wight Steam Railway. First held in 2006, staged in a marquee at Havenstreet Station (PO33 4DS). Features beers from the island's breweries as well as farther afield. A real ale bar is often open at other special events. Tel. 01983 882204. www.iwsteamrailway.co.uk

Rail Ale Festival, Welsh Highland Railway. Held since 2005, the main venue is a stone-built Goods Shed at Dinas Station. Pubs near the route of this scenic narrow-gauge line, including the Snowdonia Park brewpub at Waunfawr (q.v.), often participate. Welsh beers are prominent. Tel. 01766 516000. www.festrail.co.uk

Real Ale, Cider and Jazz Festival, Swindon & Cricklade Railway. This is sometimes held in June. Tel. 01793 771615. www.swindon-cricklade-railway.org

Real Ale Weekend (CAMRA), Gloucestershire Warwickshire Railway. Also held in September. Tel. 01242 621405. www.gwsr.com

Opposite: *The Rail Ale Festival at Barrow Hill Roundhouse in Derbyshire (May).*

JUNE

Beer Festival, Nene Valley Railway, Wansford Station. Additional trains operate and there is a bus service from Peterborough. Tel. 01780 784444. www.nvr.org.uk

Real Ale Festival, Bitton Station, Avon Valley Railway. Due to its popularity, advance booking is usually required for this event which takes place at a restored former Midland Railway station between Bristol and Bath (also in November). Tel. 0117 932 5538/7296. www.avonvalleyrailway.org

Real Ale and Cider Festival (CAMRA), Kent & East Sussex Railway, Tenterden. First held in 2009, the main venue is a marquee at Tenterden Station, and attendees can take their drinks on the platform and beside vintage Pullman carriages. Cask beers and cider are also served on some of the steam hauled services. Tel. 01580 765155. www.kesr.org.uk www.camra-afrm.org.uk

The CAMRA Real Ale & Cider Festival at the K&ESR's Tenterden Town Station, Kent (June).

Visitors to the North Norfolk Railway's Beer Festival (July) enjoy their drinks on Sheringham Station.

JULY

*Rail Ale Festival, Cleethorpes Coast Light Railway. Held at Lakeside Station. Often coincides with the Lincolnshire resort's carnival. Tel. 01472 604657. www.cleethorpescoastlightrailway.co.uk

*Esk Valley Music and Ale Train. Runs on the National Rail route from Whitby to Middlesbrough and return, on Fridays until early September. Live music with a real ale bar, usual fares apply. Tel. 01947 601987. www.eskvalleyrailway.co.uk

Beer Festival, North Norfolk Railway (The Poppy Line), Sheringham Station. Marked its 10th anniversary in 2011, this large festival occupies the length of platform two, with a rake of passenger coaches stabled alongside for seating. Focuses on beers from the Midlands, Norfolk and North East England. A frequent service of steam and diesel heritage trains operates. All proceeds go towards the railway's upkeep. Tel. 01263 820800. www.nnrailway.co.uk

Rails and Ales (CAMRA), The Battlefield Railway, Shackerstone Station, Leicestershire. A weekend of steam and real ales on the former Ashby and Nuneaton Joint Railway, including some served in Shackerstone Station booking hall and on board trains. Bosworth battlefield is at the end of the line. Tel. 01827 880754. www.battlefield-line-railway.co.uk

Ale on the Rail Weekend, Cholsey & Wallingford Railway. Ale from local breweries, served on board the trains. Main line connection at Cholsey. Tel. 01491 835067. www.cholsey-wallingford-railway.com

The driver of heritage diesel 25 057 jokes with customers at the North Norfolk Railway' Beer Festival, Sheringham (July).

AUGUST

Rails and Ales Real Ale Festival, Staverton Station, South Devon Railway. (Bank Holiday weekend). Cider also features. Run by the Devon Diesel Society and Staverton Preservation Group in a beautifully maintained location. Tel. 0843 3571420. www.southdevonrailway.org

Rail'n'Ale, Mid Suffolk Light Railway, Brockford Station, Wetheringsett, near Stowmarket, Suffolk. Annual festival with up to eight ales in the Middy Bar (q.v.) on this re-created Edwardian light railway. Tel. 01449 766899. www.mslr.org.uk

SEPTEMBER

*Shepherd Neame Spitfire Train. Annual main line steam hauled excursion from London to Faversham Hop Festival with the Faversham brewery's bar on board serving draught ale. In celebration of the hop-pickers that travelled annually from London to help with the harvest. Tel. 01795 542285. www.shepherdneame.co.uk

*Chappel Beer Festival (CAMRA), East Anglian Railway Museum. Long established (26 years) festival held in and around the railway yard and rolling stock adjacent to Chappel & Wakes Colne Station, Essex. Tel. 01206 242524. www.earm.co.uk or www.essex-camra.org.uk

Great Central Railway Beer Festival, Loughborough Station. Previous festivals have included ales selected from along the route of the 'last main line' from Sheffield to London. Tel. 01509 632323. www.gcrailway.co.uk

CAMRA Beer Festival, Bridgnorth Station, Severn Valley Railway. Long established festival in a marquee adjacent to the station. Tel. 01299 403816. www.bridgnorthcamra.org.uk

CAMRA Beer Festival, Minehead Station, West Somerset Railway, Somerset. More than a hundred ales plus local cider and perry are served at this ex-GWR terminus. Established for 12 years. Tel. 01643 704996. www.west-somerset-railway.co.uk

Autumn Steam Gala and Real Ale Festival, Bodmin General, Bodmin & Wenford Railway. Intensive service, with evening and other special trains and plenty of steam. Tel. 01208 73555. www.bodminandwenfordrailway.co.uk

Jazz, Steam and Real Ale Festival, Rushden Transport Museum, Northamptonshire. In the period setting of a Midland Railway Station of 1894 on the former Wellingborough to Higham Ferrers branch. Heritage trains run. Voted National Club of the Year 2010 by CAMRA members. Tel. 01933 318988. www.rhts.co.uk

OCTOBER

Beer and Music Festival, Keighley & Worth Valley Railway. 120 ales and a variety of live music. Tel. 01535 645214. www.kwvr.co.uk.

Ripley Rail Ale Festival (CAMRA), Midland Rail Centre, Butterley Station, Derbyshire. The first Amber Valley Beer and Cider Festival was held here in 2010 in a marquee and on board a Mark I Restaurant Miniature Buffet and Brake Gangway Car. Home to all things Midland Railway related. In Ripley is the Talbot Taphouse, brewery tap for Amber Ales. Tel. 01773 747674. www.midlandrailwaycentre.co.uk

NOVEMBER

*Swindon Beer Festival (CAMRA). Major festival held in the former Great Western Railway workshops, now part of 'Steam' Museum with its important GWR collection. www.swindoncamra.org.uk

APPENDIX III
STOP PRESS

Establishments opened or visited while this book was in production.
Future updates will be posted on www.facebook.com/railwaypubs

CANTERBURY WEST, KENT

Former South Eastern Railway between
Ashford International and Minster.

The Goods Shed, Station Road West, CT2 8AN. Tel. 01227 459153. A permanent farmers' market is held in this Grade II listed, brick-built railway shed. Beer enthusiast Andrew Morgan runs the Bottle Shop stall, stocking some 250 bottled beers and others racked in mini-casks, to drink in or take home. After 6pm the stall remains open to serve customers of the Goods Shed Restaurant. Tuesday to Saturday midday – 11pm, Sunday midday - 4 pm. www.bottle-shop.co.uk

CYMMER AFAN, NEATH & PORT TALBOT
(line and station closed)

Rhondda & Swansea Bay Railway (GWR) between
Port Talbot and Treherbert.

The Refreshment Rooms, The Old Station, Cymmer, Neath & Port Talbot, SA13 3HY. Tel. 01639 850901. Three-room pub, with restaurant extension, in stone-built station with outdoor seating on platform. Attractive 'alpine' valley location; real ale, garden, Sunday lunches a speciality. A scenic walk follows the track-bed of the South Wales Mineral Railway to Glyncorrwg in Afan Forest Park. Daily 11am – midnight.

DINGWALL, HIGHLAND

Former Highland Railway (LMS) between Inverness
and Thurso/Wick and Kyle of Lochalsh.

The Mallard, Station Square, Dingwall, Highland, IV15 9JD. Tel. 01349 866286. A spacious, single-bar pub in a shiplap building on the down (Wick/Thurso) platform. Adjacent to, but post dating the main, B Listed station building of 1886 in ashlar stone, with its ridge-and-furrow platform canopy. Large island bar counter, raised dining area, ambient music, sports screens, outside seating on platform. No real ale, meals served. Daily 10am – 1am (Sun. opens noon). In the main station building is a separate, traditional Tea Room (Mon. – Sat. 10am – 4pm, tel. 01349 865894) set with flower-decked tables; also platform seating. A brass plaque recalls that almost 135,000 sailors and soldiers were supplied from a tea stall run by the Red Cross between 1915 and 1919.

GLENFINNAN, HIGHLAND

Former North British Railway, Mallaig extension of West
Highland Railway, between Fort William and Mallaig.

Glenfinnan Station Museum, Glenfinnan, Inverness-Shire, PH37 4LT. Tel. 01397 722300. A tea-shop (unlicensed) in a restored Mark I 'Tourist Open Second' carriage is a highlight of a museum based in and around a 'Swiss-chalet' style station of 1901. Home-made cakes, light meals and hot and soft drinks are served, and there are occasional evening dinners, when guests may bring their own wine. Outdoor veranda with tables. Busy when the 'Jacobite' steam train calls during the season. Glenfinnan Viaduct and Bonnie Prince Charlie monument are within walking distance. Daily (May to late October) 9am – 4pm.   www.glenfinnanstationmuseum.co.uk

LEEDS, WEST YORKSHIRE

Former LMS and LNER, various routes.

The Hop, The Dark Arches, Granary Wharf, Dark Neville Street, Neville Street, LS1 4BR. Tel. 0113 2439854. Beneath the station, in cavernous railway arches adjacent to the Leeds & Liverpool Canal, a modern bar on two levels, opened in 2010. Central, 'Gothic style' counter and cosy seating bays. Contemporary murals decorate the walls but original brickwork is much in evidence. Ambient music and regular live bands. An Ossett Brewery pub serving up to five of the company's and up to five guest ales, usually from Yorkshire, plus real cider; pie and mash a speciality. There is a door policy on Leeds United match days. Daily, noon – midnight. www.thehopleeds.co.uk

LONDON KING'S CROSS

Terminus of the East Coast Main Line (former Great Northern Railway); also interchange with London Underground (King's Cross/St Pancras).

The Parcel Yard, Upper Concourse (adjacent platform 9), Goods Way, London N1C 4AH. Tel. 020 7713 7258. Labyrinthine, wood-floored pub belonging to London brewer Fuller's, opened in March 2012 at the same time as an eye-catching new station concourse by John McAslan. Occupies the Grade I listed GNR parcels office, an integral part of Lewis Cubitt's station of 1852, with some original features retained. Claimed by the brewery to be the 'largest station pub in the country', it has two floors with a long bar counter on each, set around a paved, double-height atrium, revealing heavy triangular roof trusses. Originally the floors were suspended from these, obviating the need for supporting columns, so horses and carts could manoeuvre easily below. Decoration includes luggage racks, railway signs and vintage brewery posters. There are six hand-pumps on each bar, mainly serving the company's ales, including London Pride and ESB, plus a guest from an independent brewer such as Adnams. Also a good wine list and food menu served until 10pm. Train departure screens. Daily 8am – 11pm. www.fullers.co.uk

TINTERN, MONMOUTHSHIRE
(line and station closed)

Wye Valley Railway (GWR) between Chepstow and Monmouth (Troy).

Carriages Tea Room, The Old Station, Tintern, NP16 7NX. Tel. 01291 689566. Tea-shop (unlicensed) set in the waiting room of this stone-built station. The expansive former station area, which also retains its stone and timber signal box and water tower, now forms part of a riverside park including a circular walk. Meals, freshly ground coffee and home-made cakes. Daily 9.30am – 5.30pm, Easter to end October. www.monmouthshire.gov.uk/oldstationtintern

BIBLIOGRAPHY

Barnes, Peter, *Traditional Pubs of Old Lancashire*, Ammanford, Sigma Press, 1992.

Betjeman, John, *Metro-Land* (DVD of 1973 BBC television broadcast), BBC Worldwide, 2006.

Biddle, Gordon, *Britain's Historic Railway Buildings*, Oxford University Press, 2003. *Great Railway Stations of Britain*, Newton Abbot, David & Charles, 1986. *The Railway Heritage of Britain* (with Nock, O.S.), Michael Joseph, 1983.

Bradley, Simon, *St Pancras Station*, London, Profile Books, 2007.

Brown, Pete, *Man Walks into a Pub*, London, Macmillan 2003, revised 2010.

Clarke, John M., *The Brookwood Necropolis Railway*, Oxford, Oakwood Press, 1995.

Ferneyhough, Frank, *The Liverpool and Manchester Railway 1830-1980*, Robert Hale 1980.

Gamston, David (editor), *Yorkshire's Real Heritage Pubs*, St Albans, CAMRA, 2011.

Hart, Brian, *The Hawkhurst Branch*, Didcot, Wild Swan Publications, 2000.

Hebron, Chris de Winter, *Dining at Speed: A Celebration of 125 years of Railway Catering*, Kettering, Silver Link Publishing, 2004.

Levisham Station Group, *Grosmont Station, A Brief History*, Pickering, North Yorkshire Moors Railway, 2007/2010.

Macdermot, E.T., *History of the Great Western Railway*, Shepperton, Ian Allan, 1927 revised 1964.

Mitchell, W.R. *Settle-Carlisle Railway*, Clapham (via Lancaster), Dalesman Books, 1979. *Shanty Life on the Settle-Carlisle Railway*, Settle, Castleberg Publications, 2004.

Peaty, Ian P., *Brewery Railways*, Newton Abbot, David & Charles, 1985.

Protz, Roger (editor), *Good Beer Guide 2010, 2011, 2012,* St Albans, CAMRA Books, 2009-12.

Ross, David, *The Highland Railway*, Stroud, Tempus Publishing, 2010.

Slaughter, Michael (editor), *Scotland's True Heritage Pubs*, St Albans, CAMRA, 2007.

Thomas, John, *The West Highland Railway*, London, Pan Books, revised 1970.

Thomas, David St John (and Whitehouse, Patrick), *The Great Days of the Country Railway*, Newton Abbot, David & Charles, 2002.

Timms, Peter, *In and Around Swindon Works 1930-60*, Swindon, self-published, 2009/10.

Veitch, Bryan, *Railway Inn Signs Book One*, Meridian Books, 2000.

Wooler, Neil. *Dinner in the Diner: The History of Railway Catering*, Newton Abbot, David & Charles, 1987.

Cast-iron BR notice in the gentlemen's toilet at Slough in the 1970s.